# POMSKIES

## A Guide for New Dog Owners

*David Anderson*

# TABLE OF CONTENTS

# CHAPTER 1

## What is a Pomsky?

Photo:
Anthony Corrigan

er body while his sister has longer legs and bigger body. She also has the duel layer "Husky fur"; a course outer layer of fur and the soft white under coat that sheds non-stop. Coco has the best of every feature. He has blue eyes, a Husky mask, and markings short legs/ small body and beautiful chocolate brown and white Pomeranian style coat that hardly sheds at all.

F2 Pomskies are a result of mating two F1 Pomskies together, which will pretty much guarantee a litter of small blue eyed Pomskies (if their parts have those features). However they do still have the DNA off both breeds, and just as we as humans can look like our grandparents, Pomskies can as well. It's just far less likely with the offspring of two F1 Pomskies."

" Not all Pomskies are small, have blue eyes, and fluffy fur, at least not F1 Pomskies (Husky-Pomeranian cross). Remember they are a cross of two breeds with different features and can get the majority of their features from either side. My Coco has Short legs and small-

*Anthony Corrigan*

Congratulations, dear reader! You want to bring with you the joy of a dog into your home. In particular, you have chosen a young Pomsky puppy, an adorable and loveable creature. Dogs are wonderful gifts given to us but are also a great source of responsibility.

Bringing home a new puppy can be an exciting and heartwarming experience. Speaking as a long time dog lover, there is no unconditional love like the love shown by a dog raised in an affectionate and devoted home. Owning a dog can be rewarding for a new pet owner. There is a lot that I have learned throughout the years while owning dogs. Dogs are great teachers of loyalty, trust, love, and compassion.

Photo: Anthony Corrigan

While it is a new experience and can be daunting in learning to care and train a young dog, it can be worth it in the long run. The following chapters serve to prepare the new dog owner, the reader, with what to expect in bringing a Pomsky puppy home. Its purpose is to help the reader in basic training and becoming familiar with the breed.

# Introduction

Pomskies are argued, by many, to be the most adorable new breed of dog that has been created. It is also, less commonly, referred to as a Huskeranian by some people. A pomsky is a cross of the Siberian Husky and the Pomeranian. It is a newer **designer dog breed** that is known for its adorable appearance, its small size, and its uncanny resemblance to a Siberian Husky. However, their appearances are very unpredictable. The Pomskies can get their appearances and temperaments from their Pomeranian parent or their Siberian Husky parent. Many people may confuse this new breed of dog with the Finnish Lapphund as Pomskies closely resemble the Finnish Lapphund and the Siberian Husky.

This dog can live, on average, for thirteen to fifteen years. They are best for families that have older children, for single adults, or for seniors. Because of their small stature, Pomskies are capable of easily adapting to apartments or houses that have or do not have yards.

In order to eliminate problems during birth and pregnancy, special care needs to be done before breeding. It is important that during breeding, the female, or the **dam**, is the Siberian Husky, while the male, or the **sire**, is the Pomeranian. This helps to avoid any birth difficulties for the Pomeranian who would carry baby dogs that are too big for it.

The Pomsky has yet to be recognized by the **American Kennel Club**, also referred to as the AKC. The AKC is an organization that recognizes and registers breeds. They have a written standard for what should be part of a purebred dog such as appearance, size, color, fur texture, temperament, and etc. The **Pomsky Club of America** is an organization that is working on creating a breed standard for the Pomsky in hopes that one day the AKC will recognize the dog as a purebred.

# Appearance

Because it is such a new breed of dog, there is not yet a breed standard. As such, the breed is not accepted by an official breed by many kennel clubs, like the American Kennel Club.

Additionally, because they are mostly bred with Siberian Huskies and Pomeranians, the size, coloring, and coat varies greatly and is very hard to predict. Normally, Pomskies are fluffy and cuddly. They are usually white or black and gray. The desired coloring is to closely match that of the husky parent, but there are many different colors and patterns found on Pomskies. Other color combinations found on Pomskies include white, black, and a rusty red and white combination. The Pomsky's coat is normally soft and long, needing daily brushing.

Pomskies are normally smaller than their Siberian Husky parent. The weight will vary from puppy to puppy. However, the weight of the Pomsky puppy tends to be the average weight of the Pomeranian and Siberian Husky. In other words, to guesstimate your future Pomsky's weight, you would have to add the weight of the Pomeranian father and the weight of the Siberian Husky mother and divide the sum. It will not be exact, but it can prove to be a good guideline to start. For the most part, Pomskies tend to weigh between twenty and thirty pounds. Again, the individual weight of each dog can vary from Pomsky to Pomsky.

Pomskies inherit physical traits from their Pomeranian fathers and Siberian Husky mothers. Some Pomskies can inherit the coloring of their Siberian Husky mother and the fox-like face of their Pomeranian father. Pomskies will most likely have a curved tail as the Pomeranian parent and Siberian Husky parent both have curved tails.

Again, each Pomsky is different, especially as it is a newer mixed breed, or designer breed. As the breed develops, breeders can carefully select traits that they like from each breed to create the "ideal" Pomsky. This is known as **selective breeding** and will not occur over night. As the breed develops, a breed standard will be created and eventually this breed may be accepted as a recognized breed by other kennel clubs throughout the country and the world.

# Temperament

The temperaments and behaviors of Pomskies can be hard to predict, much like the dog's appearance. It is important to note, especially as a new dog owner, that all dogs and puppies are different. Sometimes, the temperaments and personalities of the puppies will resemble that of their parents. So, during breeding or when picking out your puppy, you will want to take into consideration the personality and temperament of the parents as it will foreshadow what to expect when bringing home your new Pomsky.

Many Pomskies tend to be playful and gentle with kids. They are energetic dogs with a moderate activity level. Pomskies are very smart dogs and are quick learners. They love to play but are usually quieter dogs.

As these dogs are very smart, they need a lot of play to keep them from becoming easily bored. When left to their own devices, Pomskies can be notorious chewers and they are naturally great diggers.

Sometimes Pomskies have the traits that are more desired from their Siberian Husky and Pomeranian parents such as their intelligence and loyalty. Pomskies, much like their Pomeranian and Siberian Husky parents, are very protective of their humans, or their packs, as they see their families. Pomskies can be great guard dogs and will not back down easily from a threat.

On the other hand, Pomskies can also inherit the more undesired traits from their Pomeranian and Siberian Husky parents. Such traits would include a shyness around young children. Much like their Pomeranian blood relatives, Pomskies can tend to be skittish around children. Socialization must start early and remain consistent in order to successfully raise a Pomsky that is somewhat comfortable around young children. With that said, it is also equally important that young children are also supervised during their interactions with the Pomsky puppy, even as the Pomsky grows older.

Much like their appearances, a Pomsky's personality and temperament can vary greatly and can also be dependent upon the parents. It is important to remember that each Pomsky is different and it will take time to learn the personality of your pup. Getting to know your new puppy and beginning to understand what makes him tick is one of the greatest adventures in raising a puppy.

# CHAPTER 2

# Breed History

## History of the Siberian Husky

The Siberian Husky has a long and ancient history. This dog was initially bred by the **Chukchi** people. The Chukchi people were an ancient Siberian hunting people of northeast Asia, known as Siberia. The Siberian Husky is of ancient lineage, beginning over four thousand years ago, at the very least. Its exact history is unknown for the most part, however, the Siberian Husky is one of the oldest dog breds.

The Siberian Husky was bred as an endurance sled dog. They are a sturdy breed built to do hard work and built to survive extreme cold temperatures. These dogs were raised to help the Chukchi hunters pull their bundles long distances.

In 1908, the Siberian Huskies were brought to America, more specifically, Alaska. Their intended purpose to also use their strength as sled dogs during the gold rush. Since coming to America, some of the original breed qualities, as created by the Chukchi people, have disappeared. However, some of these qualities still remain.

In 1930, the Siberian Husky was officially recognized by the American Kennel Club. In 1938, the Siberian Club of America was founded.

# History of the Pomeranian

The Pomeranian also has a long history. Similar to the Siberian Husky, the Pomeranian is also a descendent of large sled dog breeds. The closest relatives to the Pomeranian are the Norwegian Elkhound, the Schipperke, the German Spitz, the American Eskimo Dog, the Samoyed, and others of that ilk.

The Pomeranian used to weigh as much as thirty pounds and was always a popular dog. It was initially popular in Europe, most noticeably in England. In 1888, the Pomeranian started its popularity in America. The first Pomeranian that was registered in the American Kennel Club's Stud Book was a Pomeranian that went by the name of Dick. It was not until 1900 that the American Kennel Club officially recognized the Pomeranian. In 1909, the American Pomeranian Club was accepted into the AKC as a **Parent Club** for the breed.

The breed's popularity still maintains high in America today. By 1950, the Pomeranian became one of the most popular breeds in America. Still, the breed remains in the top fourteen of the one hundred fifty five accepted breeds in the American Kennel Club.

# History of the Pomsky

The beloved Pomsky is a very new breed of dog. There has been an increasing interest in designer dog breeds. Many people see the purposeful mixing of purebreds to be solely for the purpose of making a quick buck. These same people argue that these designer dogs are just **mutts** or **mongrels,** the kinds of dogs easily found at animal shelters. Others see the creation of designer breeds like the Pomsky as a wonderful creation that can soon be recognized as its own purebred breed. As of right now, most Pomskies have to be mixed with a Siberian Husky and a Pomeranian to avoid the potential of inbreeding the dogs too closely.

As the breed is still relatively new, there is not much information on them right now. Additionally, because of how new they are, Pomskies are pretty rare to come across and are very costly animals. It is not surprising to find breeders trying to sell their special and beautiful puppies for over a thousand dollars per puppy. That high of a price tag only increases when the Pomsky puppies are born with markings that resemble the Siberian Husky. The price then increases even more if the puppies end up having the striking blue eyes that are highly coveted by many dog owners interested in the Siberian Husky and now the Pomsky too.

The Pomsky originates from North America and Europe. It is also in these two places where the breed has quickly grown in popularity. However, with that said, the Pomsky's specific origin is still really unknown.

The Pomsky has yet to be recognized by the American Kennel Club. However, the **Pomsky Club of America** is looking to get this new breed recognized by the AKC in the near future. The Pomsky Club of America also works to provide reliable information about the Pomsky for new dog owners or those who are interested in learning about the breed.

Because of their short history, there is not a lot of information available about the Pomsky. Be wary, dear reader, that while searching for a breeder of a Pomsky, you find one that is trustworthy and reputable. When expecting to pay a lot of money for a new furry friend, you want to be sure that you are getting the real deal. More importantly, you want to be sure that you are purchasing a Pomsky that is healthy. Finding a breeder that you can trust is discussed in further detail in a later chapter.

# CHAPTER 3

## Choosing a Puppy

*"Even though the Pomsky is a mixed breed dog (and to some people, this is their definition as a mutt) this cross-breed is fairly expensive in price. Ranging from $1,000-$6,500+ for some breeders depending on coat/color/eye color/ size."*

*Makala Braun*

Photo: Makala Braun

## Where do I Find a Pomsky?

Pomskies, while new and rare to come across, are currently in very high demand. Their attraction is mostly due to the fact that they can easily look like very small Siberian Huskies. Sometimes, Pomskies look like smaller and fluffier versions of the large Siberian Husky breed, complete with their piercing and striking blue eyes.

Breeders for Pomskies can be found all over. Pomsky breeders can be found in countries like the United States, Canada, and parts of Europe. Many of these breeders will ship their puppies to you. However, you will want to confirm that these breeders are following all laws required when shipping dogs or other animals. You want your new pet to arrive to you safe, happy, and healthy.

Especially with technology today, the ability to research, find, and communicate with Pomsky breeders all oiver the world can be a rather simple task. Alternatively, however, it is just as easy to be scammed by "false" breeders, breeders who are not really raising true Pomsky breeders and only raise dogs that look like Pomskies, or breeders that raise puppies that may not be the healthiest dogs and ones that are weak and easily fall ill.

With that said, when researching for a breeder, be thorough. You will want to find breeders that are reputable and open to you asking them questions and willing to supply you with a plethora of pictures of the parents of the Pomskies they are attempting to sell and pictures of the Pomsky puppies as well. The Pomsky Club of America provides its website viewers with a list of breeders that they find to be trustworthy sources. Many of the breeders listed by the Pomsky Club of America have their own Facebook pages. These sites are places in which potential customers can contact them. The breeders may also post pictures of their Pomskies and list the Pomsky puppies that they have for sale.

# Finding a Reputable Breeder

Photo: Makala Braun

" *Research both Husky and Pomeranian breeds to see what "normal breed traits" are and combine the two, as you may get both personalities and traits in your Pomsky. Beware of scams when searching for a breeder, always research each breeder carefully before buying".*

### Kim Wilson

Being such a new breed, there are a lot of breeders out there that will lie to unsuspecting dog owners, claiming that they breed Pomskies when in actuality they do not. You will want to do careful research of the breeder you are interested in. When looking to contact a potential breeder for your new Pomsky puppy, be ready to ask the breeder specific questions.

First of all, there are some qualities that you will want to see in your breeder. You will want a breeder that is open to questions. If you feel that he or she seems to be evasive and trying to get around answering an important question you are trying to ask, you may want to reconsider purchasing you Pomsky puppy from this breeder. You will also want a breeder that has referrals. If other dog owners do not recommend purchasing a dog from a particular breeder, there is more than likely a really good reason as to why. Alternatively, if a lot of other dog owners rave about a particular breeder, then that may be a breeder that you will want to contact about purchasing your Pomsky puppy.

You will also want to discuss purchasing a Pomsky puppy through a breeder that is more than willing to send you pictures of the parents of your future Pomsky puppy as well as pictures of your Pomsky puppy and the litter mates. You will want to talk to a breeder that is willing to be flexible in how you pay for you Pomsky. If you are able to create a paper trail, by paying with a credit card or check. If a breeder wants you to pay with cash only, that should be a red flag to you. Often times, if you are unable to create a paper trail, it is more likely that the breeder is trying to scam you. Finally, you will want to communicate with a breeder that has the paperwork readily available to you for all of the puppies he or she is trying to sell to you. The proper paperwork will ensure that you are purchasing a dog that is what the breeder is claiming it is. In other words, the proper paperwork ensures that the Pomsky the breeder is trying to sell you was sired by a healthy Pomeranian male and birthed by a healthy Siberian Husky female. This paperwork should include all background information about the Pomsky's parents. This way you know what to expect health wise from your Pomsky and the potential temperament your Pomsky may have.

As previously mentioned, there are a few questions that you will want to ask the breeder you are contacting to learn more about the Pomsky he or she is selling you, and to verify that the breeder is a reliable one.

You will want to ask the breeders you talk to about how big the Pomsky may get when it is fully grown. Normally Pomskies weigh between twenty and thirty pounds. Sometimes Pomskies can weigh as little as fifteen pounds. The way to find out how much your Pomsky should weigh is to find the average weight between the mother and the father. In other words, you would add the weights of both parents together and divide that number by two. Because of the vast size difference, most Pomskies are at least twenty pounds. Some breeders may advertise that their Pomsky puppies will weigh only five pounds when they are fully grown. Watch out for these breeders as they are normally a scam.

You will want to ask the breeder you are talking to about the cost of their puppies. Most often times, these beautiful puppies can cost as much as two thousand dollars, even as much as three thousand five hundred dollars and sometimes more. It really depends upon the coloring, markings, size, and eye color of the puppies. The smaller the dog could be the more money it will cost. Additionally, the more like a Siberian Husky the baby Pomsky looks, the more money it will cost, and that is not taking into consideration the color of the eyes.

You will want to talk to the breeder about shipping of the Pomsky puppy. Some breeders may require that you come to pick up the Pomsky yourself, while others are willing to ship the Pomsky to you. As mentioned previously, you will want to make absolute sure that the breeder you are talking to follows the laws required when shipping live animals. You will also want to research the safety of the breeder's shipping methods and you will want to ask him or her about the length of time it will take before your puppy will arrive.

On top of all of this, you will want to ask your breeder about any necessary supplies you will need when preparing to welcome your Pomsky into your home. You will also want to talk to the breeder about the amount of shedding your Pomsky will do and how to handle the grooming rituals.

Finding a reliable breeder is vital on your search to finding yourself and your family the perfect Pomsky puppy. When you feel that you have found that Pomsky breeder that you can trust, you are ready to find the puppy to welcome into your pack and begin your next adventure with the new loving soul.

# Finding the Perfect Puppy

Photo: Makala Braun

In looking for the perfect Pomsky puppy, you will need to take into consideration the cost of the puppy, the appearance of the Pomsky that you are looking for, and the personality of the puppy.

As mentioned previously, the overall cost of Pomskies can vary between their looks, size, and their eye coloring. Pomskies are easily sold starting as low as one thousand or one thousand five hundred dollars per puppy. Pomskies with the highly coveted look of having blue eyes and husky markings can be as much as three thousand dollars. A Pomsky with husky markings, with blue eyes, and is a smaller size than other Pomskies can also cost more as it is a more highly desired look. Any Pomsky with this kind of marking sold for much less can likely be a scam and you should be cautious about buying a puppy from that specific breeder. You may want to ask for DNA proof before purchasing a Pomsky, especially if you are particularly hesitant about a breeder.

Some breeders will advertise the percentage of each breed a Pomsky is. When researching to buy a Pomsky, you may see a breeder advertise that their Pomskies are **50/50** or **25/75**. Without knowing what those ratios may mean, it could be quite confusing to some new dog owners. A Pomsky that is advertised as a 50/50 Pomsky is a Pomsky that is half Pomeranian and half Siberian Husky. Some breeders will breed a 50/50 female Pomsky with a full bred Pomeranian male. This usually is done to create a smaller Pomsky. This Pomsky will then be twenty five percent Siberian Husky and seventy five percent Pomeranian.

There are certain looks of a Pomsky that is highly desired by many, which is why there is such a high price tag on the breed that fluctuates depending on the qualities the Pomsky displays. The overall goal for breeders is to have a puppy that looks like a Siberian Husky, but is the size of a Pomeranian. There are a myriad of sizes and colors among Pomskies because of the differences between each Siberian Husky and the Pomeranians. Huskies can have a lot of different fur patterns and colors as well as a lot of different colors found in their eyes.

When looking for that perfect Pomsky puppy, you will want to understand the large number of varying puppy personalities. There are common temperaments among certain breeds, however, each puppy is different. Each puppy has his or her own personality. There are some good qualities that you will want to look for in a puppy.

One quality that you will want to see in any puppy that you are looking to welcome into your family is that the puppy is people loving. Of course, when you begin training your Pomsky, you will want to socialize him. However, socialization works to an extent. Dogs can be trained to tolerate human interactions outside of their pack, but it is sometimes easier for you as the pack leader to bring home a puppy that is genuinely happy to meet new people. You will want to find a dog that looks sincerely excited to meet you from day one. You will want to see his tail wagging happily and a face that appears relaxed with a happy expression.

Another quality that you will want to have in a puppy that you are welcoming home is a self-calming nature. You want a puppy that is able to relax himself with little to no help from the doggy parent, i.e. you. Dogs that have this quality are able quiet themselves from barking and intense excitement on their own.

You also want to find a dog that is life resilient. You want a dog that is able to adjust to stressful situations on his own. This dog should have the ability to eventually grow used to certain stimuli that can be otherwise disconcerting to other dogs.

A final quality, although there are some others that you may want to look for yourself, are that your potential puppy is able to tolerate other dogs. In other words, the dog tolerant puppy does not have any desire to attack other dogs nor is he stressed out by other dogs. This quality in a dog helps him to enjoy other dogs' company or is indifferent about other dogs being around him. For the most part, much like having a dog that is people loving, this trait can be more or less conditioned to be dog tolerant through socialization training.

While there are numerous traits highly coveted by dog breeders and dog owners in regards to owning a Pomsky, the true final desirable requirement in picking out the perfect Pomsky puppy is that you find the Pomsky puppy that you and your family falls in love with. A puppy is a long time commitment and you want to be sure that you find a dog that you can forever love.

# CHAPTER 4

# Making Your House Pomsky Puppy Proof

66 *One of the best characteristics of the Pomsky is that they are highly intelligent, which helps when you want to train them. They are also very loving dogs and are protective of one or more of their human parents, usually the person who tends to spend the most time with them. Even though they are "mini" compared to a Husky, they usually have the same strengths of the Husky! Don't let their size fool you, they are highly adventurous dogs."*

**Jacquelyn Ross**

Photo: Jacquelyn Ross

## What Does a Puppy Proofed Home Look Like?

Once you have picked your perfect new Pomsky friend, you will need to puppy proof your home in preparation for your new lifetime companion. You may be wondering: "How do I puppy proof my home?"

In puppy proofing your home, you may want to seal the hardwood floors. This can help protect your floors from puppy accidents. You will also want to keep dangerous objects away from your puppy. Such items include: breakable objects, rugs, chemicals, and certain plants. By removing these items or keeping them

Photo: Jacquelyn Ross

away from your puppy you prevent these items from being destroyed as well as preventing your Pomsky puppy from hurting himself.

Puppies need space to roam. However, it is understandable that you would not want your puppy into certain rooms, especially when you are not around. Play pens, baby gates, and other forms of gating off certain areas are great tools to use to keep your puppy in certain areas of the house. This begins to teach your puppy where he is or is not allowed to go.

As mentioned before, you want to keep certain plants away from your Pomsky puppy. Many indoor, and outdoor plants, can be toxic to your puppy. Some of the toxic plants that are normally found indoors are Dieffenbachia, Azalea, Calla Lily, and Philodendron.

Medications should also be kept out of reach of your puppy. This includes vitamins. Dogs are curious animals and very good chewers, especially breeds like Pomskies. Your Pomsky will easily be able to chew through those plastic containers and get to the medicine which could get them very sick. Trash will also need to be kept out of the reach of your Pomsky. The trash should be kept up high or in a container that is more difficult for your puppy to open.

Other hazards around your home can include rocking chairs or recliners. These pieces of furniture can be hazardous to a curious puppy's tail or legs. Window blind cords should also by tied up as they can easily cause strangulation. Additionally, chords left out and chewed by the puppy can cause burns, electric shock, or even death. To protect your puppy, you will need to tie up loose cords and keep them out of sight and out of reach of your puppy. Some ways to do this are to use spiral cable wrap, cord concealers, or even PVC pipes. These methods can keep the wires out of sight, out of reach, and out of mind for your puppy.

Fireplaces, wood stoves, and other fire or heat sources can be dangerous for your puppy as well. Ultimately you will want to keep your puppy away from fires. If your puppy is around these heat sources, you must keep a close and diligent eye on your Pomsky to keep him safe.

When walking around the house yourself, be mindful of where your puppy will go. It is quite common that your puppy will want to follow you around. So, when traveling from room to room, you must be careful when closing the doors behind you. Your puppy could easily be right behind you and you will want to avoid getting your puppy caught up when you are closing the doors.

Puppy proofing a home can be simple, but special care must also be taken. You want to have a home for your Pomsky that is welcoming and safe for him at all times.

# Foods to Keep from Your Pomsky

Dogs cannot digest all the same foods that humans can. In many instances, human foods can make a dog extremely ill and sometimes lead to death. If a dog eats foods that can make them sick they can show **toxicity symptoms**. These symptoms include vomiting and diarrhea. Vomiting is the dog's way of trying to get the toxic food out of his system. Diarrhea will dehydrate the dog's body, therefore, your dog will probably drink a lot of water which will result in the dog urinating a lot.

Toxicity can cause a dog to suffer from acute kidney failure which is life threatening. If you notice any toxicity symptoms, you will want to contact your veterinarian immediately. Other symptoms include the dog's breath may smell like urine. His gums can produce ulcers. An additional symptom is that the dog's blood pressure will increase which can ultimately put your dog into a coma.

In order to treat your dog, you will need to contact your veterinarian or pet poison control as soon as possible. You may also want to induce vomiting for most instances. Before doing so, you will want to be sure you are well informed as to how to properly induce vomiting for your dog. As long as your dog did not ingest something that was a caustic substance, such as gasoline, it should be safe to try to induce vomiting. In order to properly induce vomiting you will need to know your dog's weight, any known health issues, as well as what your dog ate, when, and how much. To induce vomiting you will need

Photo: Jacquelyn Ross

to feed your dog one teaspoon of hydrogen peroxide for every five pounds your dog weighs. Again, before doing anything like this, confirm what to do with pet poison control and your veterinarian.

As mentioned before, there are a lot of foods that humans are able to ingest but dogs are not able to. The different foods listed below are dangerous to your pet in a many different ways.

- Alcohol can cause coma or death for your dog, not that any responsible dog owner is planning on feeding their pup alcohol.

- The casing on apple seeds are very toxic to dogs. The casing contains amygdlin which releases cyanide when digested. Apples are generally safe for dogs, but be sure there are no seeds in the fruit.

- Avocados contain a substance called persin which can cause diarrhea, vomiting, and heart congestion.

- Baby food, while not the worst thing in the world to feed you dog, just cannot contain onion powder.

- Cooked bones are dangerous for your dog to ingest as the bones can easily splinter when chewed on by the dog. Raw bones are safe and actually good for the nutrition and your dog's teeth.

- Candy and chewing gum has a lot of sugar and the chemical Xylitol which can cause an over-release of insulin, kidney failure, or worse for your dog.

- Cat food is also not good for your dog to consume. It contains protein for cats, not dogs. The fat and protein found in cat food is much too high for dogs.

- Chocolate is also toxic for your dog. Chocolate has caffeine as well as theobromine and theophylline. These substances are also toxic to dogs. It can cause panting, vomiting, and diarrhea. Chocolate can also damage a dog's heart and nervous system.

- Citrus oil extracts can cause vomiting for your dog if ingested.

- Coffee, much like chocolate, is poisonous for your dog.

- Corn on the cob is dangerous as it can block a dog's intestines. This blockage can be fatal and must be surgically removes. Corn also is not always the best for your dog's digestive tract anyway.

- Fat trimming should not be fed to your dog as they can cause pancreatitis.

- Fish also are not always the best to feed your dog. Salmon and trout are the fish that must be most avoided. These fish can be infested with parasites when raw. These parasites carry bacteria that can make your dog sick and potentially kill him.

- Grapes and raisins can cause liver damage and kidney failure to your dog.

- Hops, commonly used in beers, can cause panting, increased heart rate, fever, seizures, and sometimes death if ingested by your dog.

- Human vitamins normally are dangerous for dogs, especially if they contain iron. The iron can damage the digestive system.

- Liver is okay to feed your dogs, but in very small portions. Liver contains a lot of vitamin A, which can be harmful to the dog's muscles.

- Macadamia nuts contain toxins that causes weakness in your dog as well as panting, swollen limbs, and tremors. This toxin also can damage the dog's diges- tive, nervous, and muscle system.

- Marijuana, again, not that many responsible dog owners will offer marijuana to their dog, can be harmful to a dog. Marijuana can harm a dog's nervous system, negatively affect the heart rate, and cause vomiting.

- Milk and dairy products are bad for dogs as dogs are essentially lactose intolerant.

- Mushrooms are just dangerous for dogs, much like some mushrooms can be dangerous for humans.

- Onions and chives are poisonous. Consumption of onions and chives by dogs can cause anemia and damage the red blood cells.

- Persimmons, peaches, and plums are also harmful to dogs as they can cause digestion issues. More specifically, consumption of persimmons, peaches, and plums can cause intestinal obstruction and enteritis.

- Rhubarb and tomato leaves, when consumed, can negatively affect the diges- tive, nervous, and urinary systems with dogs.

- Raw fish can cause a vitamin B deficiency. Some symptoms of such a deficiency can be a loss of appetite, seizures, and rarely death.

- Salt can cause an imbalance in electrolyte levels, dehydrate the dog, and cause diarrhea.

- String, although not really a food, it is sometimes found in food, especially some meats. If a dog consumes any string, it can easily get stuck in the dog's digestive tract.

- Too much sugar consumed by a dog can cause dental issues, obesity, and diabetes.

- Tobacco is very toxic to dogs. Consumed tobacco can cause damage to the digestive and nervous systems. It can increase the heart rate, make the dog pass out, and eventually kill the dog.

- Xylitol is basically a sugar alcohol. It is commonly found in gum, candies, baked good, and etc. It is very toxic to dogs, even in small amounts. It can harm the dog by causing low blood sugar, seizures, liver failure, and death.

- Yeast, when in and out of dough, can expand and rise in the dog's stomach. Even a little yeast can cause gas. A lot of yeast consumed can ultimately rupture the stomach and intestines of the dog.

As there are a lot of human foods that are considered dangerous to dogs, it is important to keep human foods away from dogs as much as possible. If something is accidentally ingested, you will want to contact your veterinarian immediately to discuss with him or her the best course of action.

# Proper Fencing for Your Yard

Proper fencing for your yard is a great method to keep your dog or dogs in the yard while keeping other dogs out. Full fencing can also provide for great privacy for you and your family. It is a great way to manage your yard, your privacy, and your pets. It allows you to use your yard while keeping all family members safe. This includes children, pets, and etc.

There are many forms of fencing for your yard. Some forms of fencing include solid wood, chain link, farm fence, iron or aluminum, invisible, vinyl, plastic, or others.

Advice for new owners:

" *You need to have a fence. They love to be outside, especially in the winter."*

**Carmelle McHarg**

Some fencing comes with its own issues as well as benefits. Your dog can still be hyperaware of strangers passing by, your dog can easily dig under the fence, your dog can jump the fence, your dog can find ways out of the fencing, and other issues included. However, there are many ways to help keep your yard and your pet safe, even when you own a Houdini of a dog.

One way to fence your yard with an escape artist dog is through tricky landscaping. You could place shrubbery around the fence to keep the dog away from the fence. This will help to prevent the dog from being able to jump over or even dig under the fence. It ultimately keeps the dog away from the fence altogether, also discouraging the dog from barking at people who walk by.

Garden fencing, slats, or bamboo or reed rolls are another way to properly fence in the yard. These tools help to keep the dog from seeing through the chain link fencing. Without being able to see outside of the fence, the keeps the dog from becoming anxious and also gives you more privacy.

An L-Footer is a good way to help against dogs that are diggers. The fencing is bent at a ninety degree angle against the ground. It can be buried underground, but that is not necessary. This fencing makes it so the dog is unable to dig under the fence.

A concrete footer is basically concrete that is poured along the perimeter of the fence. This also helps in preventing your dog from being able to dig under the fence and escape from your fenced in yard.

Coyote rollers are usually placed at the top of a fence. They prevent coyotes from being able to get in your yard. It is also effective in keeping your dogs from getting out of your yard.

Lean-ins are built at the top of the fencing to your yard. It is placed at an angle in towards your yard, much like an awning. This keeps the dogs from being able to jump over the fence as well.

Redundant fences are essentially a fence within a fence. They are place on one side of the yard or all around the yard. Redundant fences are used to eliminate problem areas, weak portions of an outer fence that, for some reason, cannot be fixed, or for dogs that are sticking their heads through the fencing. The redundant fencing does not have to be expensive, it just really needs to be sturdy enough for your puppy, including when your puppy gets older.

Airlocks are also a great system to have with the fenced in yard. An airlock is essentially a smaller gated area that is outside the gated area. It keeps the dogs from completely escaping if a gate is left open accidentally. It is basically a double gate. Airlocks are used at a lot of doggie day cares and animals shelters to prevent dogs from running out of the fenced in area when they should not be.

Many dog owners opt for electrical fences or hidden fences or invisible fences. These are additionally known as underground fences. This type of fencing is becoming more and more popular for dog owners. They are cheaper than other fencing to install and also preferred as they keep the yard open, which many homeowners may prefer.

Underground feces work mainly with a radio antenna that sends out a signal to the battery in the dog's collar. It does not cause a shock to the dog, but more like static electricity to keep the dog from running out of the yard. Before the dog gets to the edge of the yard, there is a warning tone that alerts the dog that he is getting too close to the edge of the yard.

This will require some training. Many dog owners use flags to mark off the boundaries. Training your puppy with a leash and collar can also be helpful. To start, you can tape off one of the prongs so the dog will only hear the sound without feeling any vibration. As your puppy returns to the safe area, where the beeping stops, praise and reward your puppy. Once your puppy is comfortable with the boundary, add distractions. You want your puppy to get used to the boundaries and you can then gradually wean your puppy off the leash and also gradually remove the flags that mark the lining.

Some disadvantages to the invisible fences are that they cannot be seen by other people. This may cause the people to become nervous about your dog running to the edge of the yard, trying to protect his territory from outsiders. Some dogs are also able to ignore the vibration and go through the invisible barrier. It does not work on all dogs. If it does not work with your dog, you will have to consider a different option from the invisible fence. This type of fencing also needs to be maintained.

# Keeping Your Pomsky Puppy Safe Outdoors

You will want your puppy to enjoy the outdoors just as much as you do. In order to help your puppy to enjoy his time outside, you want to make your yard Pomsky puppy proof.

First of all, you will want to always supervise your Pomsky when outside. When leaving your Pomsky outside, you will have to have an outdoor kennel or secure fencing. You will want the fencing structured so your puppy is unable to dig under it, jump over it, or even chew through it. You should also keep a separate area of the yard reserved specifically for your dog to use as a place to relieve himself. This will be important during potty training.

As with some plants being dangerous to dogs indoors, there are also many plants found outdoors that can be toxic to your Pomsky puppy. Some plants are potato, morning glory, foxglove, lily of the valley and oak. If allowing your puppy free to roam in your yard, you will need to either keep a diligent eye at all times with these plants in your yard, have the plants in a fenced off area of the yard, or not have these plants in the yard at all. Not having these toxic plants in your yards is the best chance to not have your pet accidentally ingest the plants and become ill.

You will also want to protect your Pomsky from water sources such as pools, ponds, hot tubs, and others. If these water sources are found in your yard, you will need to take precautions in protecting your Pomsky from such hazards.

Similarly with indoor heat sources, many homeowners enjoy having a fire pit outside to sit around, especially on warm summer nights or cool spring or fall nights. These fire and heat sources are dangerous to your Pomsky. You will need to watch him at all times while still enjoying these appliances outside in order to prevent burns on your Pomsky.

Again, you will want to cover and secure your outdoor garbage receptacles. Properly securing these receptacles will help to keep your Pomsky from getting into things he should not be. You will also want to keep an eye out and remove hazards from your yard such as nails, broken glass, or other sharp objects. You do not want your Pomsky to cut or impale himself on any sharp hazard laying around your yard.

# What do I Need to Keep out of Reach of My Pomsky?

There are a myriad of items that you will want to keep away from your Pomsky, including the long list of food mentioned earlier in the book. Many of these items are commonly found around the home and will need to be properly disposed of to protect your Pomsky from getting sick. Some of these items are listed below.

Baby diapers are made of an absorbent material. These objects are danger-ous for your dog as they can become a blockage in the dog's stomach and intes-tines. Another dangerous and absorbent material for your dog to digest are many feminine products.

Anti-freeze has an ingredient that can taste sweet, but when ingested can cause kidney failure. Additionally, pest control products are very toxic for your dog to consume. While the products are created to be attractive for pests to con-sume, your beloved Pomsky may be drawn to the poisonous product. When using them, make absolute certain that you put it in a place that is impossible for your dog to get to and ingest. This will keep your puppy safe.

Sago palms are also toxic to a dog's liver. When ingested, this can cause liv-er failures. Foxtails are a weed that is normally found in the western half of the United States and is very toxic to all dogs.

# CHAPTER 5

# The First Few Days with Your Pomsky Puppy

## Preparing the Home

So, you have picked out your beautiful Pomsky and are excited to bring him home. However, are you, your family, and your home ready for your Pomsky to run amuck? You want to make sure that you have the proper supplies necessary for your young puppy.

Photo: Lexi Wo

You will need puppy gates. You want to be able to keep your puppy out of areas that can be dangerous to them or your belongings. A lot of puppies are curious and need to be kept in areas that will keep them out of trouble, especially when they are not able to be supervised.

You will also need dog bowls for food and water. If you get stainless steel bowls, it will keep your puppy from chewing through the bowls. Heavy bottoms to the bowls will also help by making it difficult for the puppy to knock over the bowls, spilling food and water everywhere.

You will want to have leashes, collars, harnesses, and chew toys for your puppy before you take him home. Chew toys must be safe for your puppy. You can check with your veterinarian to find toys that are safe to give to your puppy. The toys must be durable and non-toxic. Keep in mind that you do not want the toys to be too tough for your puppy's teeth.

You will want a crate for your Pomsky as well. You will be able to use for crate training in the house and/or as a travel crate. Any crate that you purchase for your Pomsky you want to make sure that it is big enough for your puppy to be able to twist and turn.

There is a lot going on the first few days that your puppy is welcomed home. You will want to be mindful of the fact, while it is an exciting day for you, it will be a very stressful day for your Pomsky. Your puppy has been brought to a new environment, new people, and new smells, without any of his littermates or mother.

To help your puppy with the transition in his new home, you will need to set rules for your puppy and the rest of your family. Your puppy has a new family or a new pack, therefore, he has to learn a new set of rules and expectations of his new family.

Be mindful of the fact that your puppy will be nervous. You will need to demonstrate a lot of patience with your young puppy. He will also need to learn to trust you as he finds a place in his new pack.

You can also help out your puppy by separating areas for specific needs. You need to provide an area for your Pomsky puppy to sleep. This would include a dog beg and a toy. You want your puppy to feel comfortable and cozy in his new home from day one. You will also want to have a separate area for your puppy to eat. An area for the puppy to use the bathroom is also important, especially when beginning potty training.

You also want to have an area that is safe to keep your Pomsky when supervision is not readily available. This area could be a crate, large enough for him to move around freely, or contained by a play pen or baby gates.

In preparing your home for your new family member, you will want to create an environment for your puppy that is warm, welcoming, comfortable, and makes him feel safe. Coming home for the first time is an exciting time for you and the other members of your family. At the same time, it is a stressful time for your Pomsky puppy. You will need to be patient with him as he adjusts to his new surroundings and learns to trust you and the rest of his new pack. It will be worth it all in the long run as you gain a most loyal friend.

# Preparing the Kids

If you have children, you know how excited they will be when they learn that a new puppy will be joining their family. It is important that you properly prepare your children for how to care for a puppy without overwhelming the puppy. You want to always supervise your children around your Pomsky, especially as some Pomskies can tend to be anxious around younger children. This will take continuous socialization, but we will discuss that in further depth later.

Photo: Karen McCullough

One way to help teach your children responsibility in taking care of a puppy is by setting a schedule with your dog and your children. A schedule helps to keep your children and the puppy understand expectations. A schedule helps the puppy to relax as he learns the routine. He will understand how his new pack runs and his place in the new pack. A routine helps to teach your children what to do to properly care for your puppy.

You will want to schedule how often your puppy is fed. For puppies that are younger than six months should be fed about three times a day. Older dogs should be fed two times per day. Scheduled bathroom breaks will be based off of the feeding schedule. You will also want to work with your children to schedule walking times.

Play times must also be structured as to where the puppies can play and for how long. Play time should be at least twenty minutes per day. The play time includes training. You will want your children involved in the training sessions. This will help them learn how to work with the new puppy and the puppy will learn that he needs to listen to all of the humans in the pack. Remember, you should always supervise your children while they spend time with the new puppy.

In preparing your children, you will want to teach your children how to respect dogs. You want to warn children against being too rough with your puppy. Such roughness can include rough play, allowing the children to pull the dog's ears, smothering the puppy with hugs, poking at the puppy, climbing on the puppy and etc. These actions can scare the puppy, hurt the puppy, or the puppy can end up unintentionally hurt your child because he is hurt or afraid.

Before your puppy comes home, preview good interactive behaviors with the puppy before bringing the puppy home. You can sometimes demonstrate polite behaviors with a stuffed toy so your child knows how to interact with the puppy before it comes home and feels more welcome.

Some basic rules that you will want to teach your children are to never take an object from a dog. You want the child to know to not disturb a dog while he is sleeping or eating. Encourage your child to avoid sneaking up on the dog. A dog should be allowed to smell the hand of the child, or anyone, before being petted. You should warn your child that growling, barking, or staring into a dog's eyes can be seen as a threat. You want to also encourage your child to not be afraid of telling a parent or trusted adult if the puppy shows any aggressive tendencies.

# The Ride Home with Your New Puppy

precionspomskies.com

Photo: Lexi Wo

You are ready to bring your puppy home. You have done your research, you have picked out your puppy, and you have prepped your home and family to welcome the new addition to your pack. Now you need to pick him up to bring him home.

In your car, you will want to bring some treats, a toy, and a spare towel. You will also want to bring some cleaning supplies in case the puppy gets car sick or has an accident on the ride home. You may also want to bring another adult with you to drive the car. This will give you the opportunity to comfort and bond with the puppy on the ride home. You can talk soothingly to the puppy and poke your fingers through the crate for him to sniff. You want to make the puppy feel as safe as possible, this is a stressful time and huge change in environment for him. It is good to comfort him, but if he is excessively whining and seems overly nervous, comforting this behavior can actually make the puppy more nervous.

You want your puppy safe and secured in the car. Avoid cuddling the puppy in the car. Your arms are not as safe for the puppy in the instance of a car accident as a well secured crate could be. While secured in the crate, provide your puppy with treats and toys to keep him occupied and comforted. You will also want to avoid comforting and holding your puppy during that first car ride home because you will want to train your puppy proper car riding etiquette in the future.

# The First Night and First Few Days with Your New Pomsky

The first few days with your new Pomsky is sometimes referred to as the honeymoon period. Eventually, with all the excitement and initial training, you will quickly get tired, but that does not mean you should relax on training your Pomsky from day one.

From day one, you will want to set ground rules and maintain consistency. For example, if you do not want to have your puppy on the furniture later, you should not allow your puppy on the furniture from the beginning. Inconsistency can cause confusion for your dog.

Additionally, you want to have a set schedule that you keep consistent. If you get your dog over a weekend, you will want to schedule his bathroom breaks for times that are consistent with your work schedule during the week.

You will also want to let your puppy get used to being home alone. Crate training is a great start for this. While going on short errands, leave your puppy in the crate. This will help him get used to being in the crate or being confined to another safe area for times that you are away, especially when you get ready to go back to wrok.

In preparing for the first night and the first few days with your new Pomsky puppy, keep in mind that all puppies are different. Some puppies will waltz into your home as if they own the place and it was their home from the very start. Others may be very nervous. Some puppies will be okay and energetic during the day, however, as night falls, they may cry all night long. It is important that you practice patience with your puppy. He will need time to adjust to his new environment and new pack. It can be very stressful for him and he needs your support from day one. If your puppy seems more hesitant or shy or nervous around you, especially if he is growling, you may want to seek special help.

The first few days, let alone the first night, in his new home, can be more than stressful for the young Pomsky puppy. It is important as his new pack leader and new dog owner, you make him feel comfortable, happy, and safe. You need to give him time to adjust to his new pack. Once he is settled and comfortable your Pomsky will soon run around the house as if he owns the place, but hopefully within the guidelines you set for him.

# Taking Your Pomsky to the Veterinarian for the First Time

A trip to the veterinarian is one of the first trips you want to take with your new Pomsky puppy. A veterinarian trip should be done immediately, within the first forty eight hours of having your Pomsky puppy.

In preparation for your first trip to the veterinarian, you will want to bring any and all paperwork that your puppy came with. If you went through a reputable breeder, you should have all the paperwork required. Some breeders actually already do the vaccinations or deworming needed before letting the puppy go home with their new families.

The first trip to the veterinarian is normally a basic check-up. The veterinarian performs a physical examination. The veterinarian will do a basic go over, checking the puppy's skin, body, coat, ears, nose, and mouth. The veterinarian will check your puppy's vision, hearing, and alertness.

The initial exam also includes vaccinations, if not already taken care of by the breeder. There are four core recommended vaccines for puppies. These vaccines are **distemper, canine hepatitis, canine parvovirus,** and **rabies**. The rabies vaccine is most normally required by law across the country. There are other vaccines are needed based on where you are located and what common diseases are there.

The initial exam may also include a fecal exam and deworming. Most puppies are actually born with roundworm and deworming medication will be given at home or during the first veterinarian if he has roundworm.

The veterinarian will also help with flea and tick prevention. Fleas and ticks can be annoying to dogs but more importantly can carry diseases. Your veterinarian will knw what type of medication is needed to protect your pet from these parasites.

**Microchipping** can be a very important part of your puppy's first trip to the veterinarian. Microchipping is a process in which a small identification tag is inserted into the dog. The microchip itself is really small, the size of a grain of rice. It has the dog's information and your contact information. If you are to ever lose your dog and your dog is found, his chip is able to be scanned. It helps to bring your dog home to you sooner. Microchipping is a low cost and simple procedure. It is simply injected between the shoulder blades of your dog. Even with the microchip, you will want to have a collar and identification tag on your dog at all times. You also want to be sure to register all of your information with your dog's microchip to ensure that he finds his way home to you sooner.

During your first visit you will want to ask plenty of questions. You are going to an expert in the field. He will be able to give you answers and help you feel more confident as a new dog owner.

The first visit to your veterinarian can be hectic. There is a lot of noise, distractions, and smells. It can be stressful for you and your puppy. To alleviate that stress on your new puppy, be open and calm. You should realize that your puppy feeds off of your energy. Your calm energy will help to relax your puppy. Allow the visit to the veterinarian to be a relaxing and informative experience. The trip to the veterinarian should not be a scary experience for your puppy. Try and help your puppy to realize that it is something that will make him feel better or keep him healthy. It is important to visit your veterinarian on a regular basis.

# Pomsky Puppy Class

Photo: Margaret Schmucker

When training your Pomsky, you may want to consider enrolling him in a **puppy class**. The puppy classes and training in general should be started at a young age for your Pomsky. The purpose of these puppy classes are to help teach your Pomsky proper puppy manners. The training portions should be short and quick as there is a lot of information for the Pomsky puppies to retain and they can easily become distracted by the other puppies around them.

These puppy classes can teach your puppy a lot. Many lessons taught during puppy classes include lessons on giving your puppy confidence in himself, lessons on not biting, lessons on socialization with other dogs and other people, and lessons on being comfortable with being handled by strangers. When your puppy is comfortable with being handled by strangers, visits to the veterinarian will become much easier in the near future. Puppy classes also work on your new Pomsky's ability to respond to different verbal cues such as sit, come, lie down, stand, stay, and others, without being distracted and without being given a reward all the time.

It is important that you research carefully the type of puppy class that you are planning to sign your Pomsky up for. Some puppy classes can prove to not be as beneficial or helpful for your Pomsky as they advertise. Careful selection of a puppy class is advised.

There are some characteristics of a good puppy class that you will want to look for when doing your research and making a final decision. You will want a class that keeps the puppies off their leashes during the entire session, with the exception of when there is a lesson in which the puppies are taught to walk on a leash. You will want a puppy class that is mostly spent off the leash because it is important to know how to control your Pomsky puppy when he is not on a leash. There are more times during your everyday life in which your Pomsky will be off the leash such as times while at home and while at the dog park. You cannot learn how to control your puppy when he is off the leash when you are training him on the leash. Alternatively, your Pomsky will not learn that he should be listening to you at all times and not just when he is on the leash.

The time in the class should not be spent with your Pomsky on the leash and the trainer talking. This is a waste of precious time that could and should be spent working on obedience with your Pomsky. A lot of the time spent during these puppy classes should actually be spent with the puppies learning by playing. It is great for their socialization and provides a lot of supervision. Puppies have short attention spans so the play time should be interrupted frequently and in small spurts. When play time and training are combined, training becomes enjoyable for your Pomsky. When your puppy enjoys his training lessons, he is able to retain more of the information that given to him.

Furthermore, interrupting the continuous play time to work on different commands can often times help to teach the puppies to focus and when it is time to listen to their owners. This can come in handy when you take your Pomsky to play dates or the dog park and is lost in the play time. When it is time to go or you need to pull your dog away for whatever reason, it is important that your dog will listen to you regardless of what he is currently focused on.

You also want to have a trainer running your puppy class that is able to resolve any sort of fearfulness and bullying that may come up in the class. Because the puppy classes involve puppies of all different breeds, sizes, personalities, and play style, there can be some puppies who try to dominate the play and other puppies who are fearful of the other, more dominant puppies. The trainer running the puppy classes should be knowledgeable enough to stop any sort of bullying or overly rough play during the puppy classes.

*Photo: Lexi Wo*

Puppy classes are great experiences for you to sign your puppy up for. They can help with early socialization for your puppy. These classes can also help to teach basic obedience to your Pomsky puppy. You will want to enroll your Pomsky early and start from day one. Find a puppy class that is well organized and run by a trainer who is competent in running a class filled with young puppies. And remember, these classes should be fun for the puppies. If the training is fun, you Pomsky will tend to absorb more of the information.

# CHAPTER 6

# The First Few Weeks with Your Pomsky Puppy

## Setting Boundaries

Once your puppy has been brought to his new home, you will need to set firm boundaries from day one. Furthermore, you will need to be consistent with these boundaries. You will also want to work to build a bond with your Pomsky. Dogs are pack animals, it is in their blood. This pack mentality and forging a bond with your Pomsky will help to teach your puppy his place in the pack.

Puppies, when first brought home, will try to test their boundaries. As the pack leader, it is your job to set the boundaries, much like your puppy's mother would. These boundaries include where the puppy can sleep, where the puppy can use the restroom, and where the puppy can eat.

In the wild, packs are ruled by the **alpha** male and female. The alpha is normally chosen by being the strongest and the bravest in the pack. The alpha male decides where the pack will hunt, where the pack will sleep, who will eat and when. The alpha female is in charge of the other females and the pups in the pack. She normally is in charge of the discipline of the puppies.

Setting boundaries will help your Pomsky puppy focus during training. It will help when he is learning how to properly walk on a leash, when he is learning how to act around people and other animals, and when he is learning where he is allowed in the house and around the yard.

In order to be happy and healthy puppies that grow into well balanced dogs, dogs need to know what they can and cannot do. You will need to set these boundaries right away. You should keep consistent tones of voice when setting these boundaries with your Pomsky. You will want the tones and sounds you make to convey what is and what is not acceptable behavior from your Pomsky. When your puppy leaves an area he is not supposed to be in or stops doing what he should not be doing then, in order to convey he has made a good decision, you should praise him. You may want to also set up doggie gates or baby gates in order to keep your Pomsky away from areas that you do not want him to be in.

Setting boundaries are beyond vital to raising a happy and healthy Pomsky. These boundaries will help your Pomsky learn his place in his new pack. Your Pomsky has been brought from his litter and home, to a new place with new people and new smells. He is unaware of the rules he is supposed to follow in his new home. It is your job as his new alpha to teach him these rules by setting those boundaries.

# Socializing Your Puppy Right Away

You will want to begin socialization with your puppy from day, as soon as you bring your Pomsky puppy home. The longer you wait to socialize your puppy, the harder it becomes.

In fact, dogs are most understanding of new things when they are between three and twelve weeks of age. This is the prime time in which you will be able to introduce your Pomsky to new people, new dogs, new sounds, new sights, new smells, and children. After the twelve weeks, your puppy becomes more cautious of new experiences.

By twelve to eighteen weeks, socialization is still possible with your puppy. However, it becomes even harder to socialize your puppy. After eighteen weeks, it is almost impossible to introduce your puppy to anything new.

More will be explained later on in the book about how to properly socialize your puppy to different experiences. But here, it is important to realize that socialization is important to raise a dog that is well adjusted to other dogs, other people, and new experiences. This socialization, in order to be successful, must start from day one.

# Treats and Rewards Training

Many trainers use treats and rewards for successful training sessions and when the dogs perform desired behaviors. Many trainers also prefer reward training, using praise and treats, versus other methods.

When training, using treats, you must keep in mind that you may be feeding your Pomsky a lot of treats. Because of this, you may want to consider purchasing treats that are healthier for your Pomsky. There are treats that are made with peanut butter and fruits and vegetables. These treats can prove to be a good option to train your Pomsky with. Dogs are well known for their love of peanut butter. Other trainers also use small pieces of chicken treats to reward the dogs for performing a desired behavior.

Overall, treats and reward training can be highly effective in properly training your Pomsky. It has been found by many trainers that dogs respond well to reward training. If they are rewarded for performing a certain behavior, they are more likely to repeat that behavior again. Your dog not only wants the treat, but when treats are coupled with praise, your dog also wants to please you and earn your affection and praise.

# CHAPTER 7

# Housetraining

## Positive Rewarding During Training

Housetraining your puppy is one of the most important behaviors that you train your puppy to do. It is important to teach your Pomsky to use the bathroom outdoors as it helps to set the boundaries that are so important for your new Pomsky.

During training, you will want to keep in mind that sometimes a dog may have accidents inside the house because of a variety of behavioral reasons. A dog may have separation anxiety, he may be marking territory, he may be showing submission, he may also be showing excitement. Normally, your dog may have an accident inside the house because of fear, anxiety, or over stimulation and excitement.

*Photo: Lexi Wo*

Punishment and scolding your puppy for having an accident inside the house does not do much to creating a positive outcome. Instead, a positive outcome in housetraining derives from using positive reinforcements and rewarding your dog for his positive behavior.

You will want to reward your Pomsky puppy for using the bathroom in an appropriate area and when he is able to eventually acknowledge the fact that he has to use the bathroom and finds his own ways to let you know. You will want to watch your puppy to learn the signs that he gives that demonstrates when he needs to use the bathroom.

Photo: Karen McCullough

It is important to avoid scolding your puppy for accidents. If you scold him for having an accident in the house, you run the risk of making your Pomsky fearful of you and going to the bathroom. In fact, if you scold your Pomsky for having an accident in the house, he may end up believing that he should not use the bathroom at all in front of people and will tend to hide whenever he needs to go to the bathroom. If your Pomsky has an accident in the house, do not make it a big deal. Silently clean the area up without acknowledging the mess. You should be patient and carry a calm demeanour.

When you take your Pomsky outside to relieve himself, leave him be. This will allow him to focus on the task at hand. Give him a few minutes to focus on what he needs to do and to settle and use the bathroom. Immediately after your puppy is able to relieve himself in the properly designated area, praise him with your voice, affection, and a small treat.

The timing of this reward is vital. You will need to wait until your puppy has completely finished going to the bathroom. You do not want to reach for the treats or talk to your puppy while he is settling in to relieve himself. You will need to ignore him and maintain stillness, otherwise you may end up distracting your puppy. You want to reward him right after he finishes. If you reward him too early, your puppy may not finish going to the bathroom completely. If you wait too long to praise and give your puppy the reward, he will more than likely be unable to connect the behavior of going to the bathroom with his reward.

Again, potty training or housetraining your young Pomsky puppy is very important, especially when trying to set boundaries with your pet. Positive rewarding is the best way to successfully train your Pomsky for all behaviors across the board.

# Crate Training

Crate training is helpful when housetraining your Pomsky. In fact, crate training helps to eliminate accidents in the household, especially for times when there is not any supervision available for your Pomsky, making it impossible for someone to let him out when he tries to show that he needs to use the bathroom.

The reason why crate training is so successful is because dogs do not like to use the bathroom where they are supposed to sleep and rest. If your Pomsky is placed in a crate, especially when sleeping or resting, he will avoid using the crate as a place to relieve himself.

Crates also serve as a safe place for the puppy to relax when you are busy or are unable to provide him with the supervision he needs. Keep in mind, however, that you do not want to keep your Pomsky in his crate for long, extended periods of times. He will need to be able to move around on his own, around your home. And quality time with your Pomsky pup is priceless.

The crate you buy for your Pomsky has to be the perfect size for him. It needs to be large enough for him to be able to comfortably stand, turn around, lie down, or stretch out in the crate. However, the crate must also not be so large that the puppy will end up finding a corner where he can relieve himself.

Crate training is a great method to teach your Pomsky to use the bathroom in a designated area. Because of the natural instinct of not wanting to use the bathroom where he sleeps, keeping your Pomsky in his crate, when you are out of the house and unable to supervise him, will help to train him to hold it until you are around and can bring him to the designated bathroom area. Positive reinforcement is the best way to properly train your Pomsky to be housetrained. Housetraining is a very important behavior for your Pomsky to learn and with the proper tools, you can set him up for success.

# Setting a Schedule

Much like you set boundaries for your dog day one, you will also want to set a schedule for your dog. You want to be consistent with this routine or schedule as it will make housetraining much easier for you and your loveable pooch.

Start by showing your Pomsky puppy a place where he can go to the bathroom. Puppies and dogs like to use areas that are absorbent to relieve themselves on, much like a rug. You want to avoid allowing your dog to use these surfaces to go to the bathroom and demonstrate that there is one area for him that is appropriate to relieve himself on.

You will also want to use a keyword, letting your dog know when it is time to use the bathroom. Some keywords or phrases can be simple like "Outside," "Do you have to go outside?" "Do you need to go potty?" and others. You will want to have a light hearted tone of voice, to keep the exercise welcoming and not something that makes him nervous. You will also want to use the same exit to get to the yard each time and use the same area of the yard each time. Again, when your dog is sniffing around, getting ready to go to the bathroom, you want to ignore your puppy so as to avoid distracting him.

Consistency and patience during dog training is important. In fact, repetition and consistency is the key to successful housetraining. When your dog is used to a specific routine, you are more likely to set him up for success.

Also, to help with setting a schedule, you will want to start my setting a feeding schedule for your dog. Puppies need to be fed three times a day. Adult dogs only need to be fed two times per day. A set feeding schedule helps to create a set potty schedule. You should take your young puppy out to use the bathroom ten to fifteen minutes after eating, after playing, or after waking up from a nap. Adults, on the other hand are able to hold their bladders for as much as three to four hours. Puppies can really only hold their bladders for one to two hours at a time. Therefore, frequent bathroom breaks are a must.

Once again, having a dog that is housetrained is one of the most important things that you can train your dog to do. Housetraining a puppy will take a lot of time and can be frustrating to new dog owners who will grow tired of cleaning up after their new puppy who is still learning. During housetraining, you will want to practice patience, encouragement, and exuding a calming demeanor in front of your dog. Avoid scolding your dog and focus more on positive reinforcement when he does something right. With patience and determination, you and your Pomsky puppy can be a very successful experience.

# CHAPTER 8

## Socializing Your Pomsky

" Your
Pomsky will have a lot
of energy, which comes
from both the Husky and
the Pomeranian. They
will need to have lots of
exercise. You need to be
aware that this is an adorable breed and you will
get stopped anywhere
you go because they
get lots of attention!"

*Makala Braun*

Photo: Lexi Wo

## Why it's Important

Socializing your Pomsky from day one is so important. Even more important is that you continue socializing your Pomsky throughout his lifetime. A socialized Pomsky can hope to become a safer and more relaxed dog. A socialized Pomsky will be more comfortable with new experiences and with meeting new people. Your Pomsky, once socialized, is also less likely to be fearful of other people. A fearful dog can tend to be dangerous to himself and to others. Ultimately, his fear can lead to aggression.

Overall, the more you socialize your puppy, the more comfortable he will be with new experiences and less apt to be fearful of new things. It is important to socialize your Pomsky because it will help you to raise a puppy that is happy, healthy, and well balanced.

# When Do I Start?

You will want to start socializing your Pomsky from day one. As previously discussed, puppies that are ages three weeks to twelve weeks are most receptive to newer experiences. Because of this, the sooner you start socializing your Pomsky, the better. After eighteen weeks old, it rapidly becomes increasingly difficult to socialize your Pomsky and ultimately it becomes nearly impossible.

Socialization is an ongoing process and should never be stopped, even when you feel as if your Pomsky is completely comfortable with new experiences you will want to still continue socializing him.

Socializing your Pomsky will also take a lot of time and patience. Socialization does not happen in one training session. Overall, you will want to expose your puppy to things that he may see every day or even on some rare occasions. Some experiences that you may want to consider exposing your Pomsky to are babies, young children, older children, other dogs, adults, cars, loud noises, other animals, and other experiences that they may come across on their daily walks with you. It is suggested that you will want to focus on commonalities, events and people and animals that your dog is most likely to come across. Again you will want to practice consistency on top of patience. Consistency will lead your puppy to being able to generalize these events and anything that they come across and able to remain calmer when around these stimuli.

During sessions in which you are socializing your Pomsky, you will want to avoid overwhelming your Pomsky. Read your dog's body language. If you notice that your Pomsky is cowering or whimpering, you will need to seriously consider giving him a break. You need to take socialization slowly with your Pomsky. The goal for socializing your Pomsky is to make your puppy comfortable about the new experiences and enjoy them, not become fearful of new experiences.

To achieve this goal, you will want to do your best to make socialization enjoyable for your puppy. You will want to make it fun for him. Use rewards and praise to build your puppy's confidence and to reward his positive behavior and reactions to the socialization. If you notice that your puppy is becoming fearful of a stimulus, take him further away from the stimulus. Do not completely leave the situation, but take him further away to lessen his stress. You will want to reward good behavior around the stressful or scary stimulus. You want to train your puppy to begin to see the stimulus as a good thing and not a negative thing. You should also avoid rewarding fearful behavior with coddling. This will only encourage your dog to be fearful of these things instead of becoming desensitized by them.

The socialization process needs to be taken slowly and patience must be exercised. You do not want to push too much on your puppy too quickly lest he begins to see new experiences as a negative thing. A well socialized puppy tends to be a confident, calm, and happy dog to be around as he grows and matures.

# Introducing Your Pomsky to Other Dogs and Animals

66 *One thing that really surprised me about my Pomsky was that I had no idea she would have such a strong prey drive. She catches and eats mice whenever she gets the chance. She will chase cats, rabbits, and squirrels. New Owners need to be aware of this if they have other small pets in the house!"*

**Carmelle McHarg**

Photo: Sheron Steele - FlyMale

Before socializing and introducing your Pomsky to other dogs and animals, you will want to ensure that your puppy is fully vaccinated. Vaccinations will help to ensure that your dog is protected by common illnesses that other animals or dogs could carry and pass onto your precious puppy. It is not only important to socialize you dog with other dogs. You will also want to consider socializing your puppy with other animals, especially ones that your dog may easily cross paths with. For example, if you know that your dog will constantly cross paths with a cat, then from day one you will want to socialize your dog with cats. Dogs that are raised around cats tend to get along with other cats in general and not seem them as prey.

Socializing your Pomsky puppy with other puppies is also important. You will want to, however, socialize your puppy with other puppies that are friendly and healthy. You do not want your puppy getting hurt or sick by playing with other puppies. Puppy classes can help with socialization as well. Other ways to help your dog socialize with other dogs is by taking frequent trips to the dog part, as long as your puppy has been fully vaccinated.

When introducing your Pomsky puppy to other dogs there are some guidelines that you will want to follow. First of all, you will want to choose a neutral place for the dogs to initially meet. One suggestion might be to bring both dogs to a dog park that is new to each of them. This neutral zone will help to avoid the dogs getting territorial, which could end up causing more problems.

You will need multiple handlers. Do not attempt to introduce two dogs by yourself. If you need to separate the dogs, you will need the other set of hands to take one dog in one direction as you take your dog in the other.

Provide a lot of positive reinforcement during the initial interactions. Allow the dogs to sniff one another and become acquainted with one another. Praise these positive interactions with happy and lighthearted tones. You will want to avoid using threatening tones throughout the entire experience. You want your dog to feel that meeting new friends are happy occasions and not scary or negative experiences.

You will also want the interactions to be short. You do not want to pressure the dogs. One dog, if over stressed, could become aggressive. To prevent this, interrupt the interactions with simple commands like sit, lie down, paw, and etc. This will keep your dog from obsessing over his new friend and getting anxious or the other dog becoming anxious.

Throughout the interaction, you will want to watch the body language of both dogs. Aggressive behavior could be displayed by a dog in numerous ways. Some ways a dog will show aggressive tendencies are by growling, staring, baring his teeth, his hair may be standing on end, referred to as **piloerection**, and walking stiffly. If either dog is displaying this sort of behavior, you will need to separate the dogs immediately and find ways to calm them down. You may ask your Pomsky to sit or lie down, for example. When both dogs have a calmer body language, reward them with treats and praise. It is possible to try the interaction again, but you will need to give each dog more space and give breaks more frequently. Eventually, the dogs should stop showing aggression. When they seem to not show any more aggression, the dogs are more likely to be more comfortable with one another and the initial introduction is done.

Introductions and socialization of your dog with other dogs is extremely important when looking to raise a well-balanced and social dog. As with other training, patience is key. It is important to take it slowly and to avoid stressing your Pomsky out by over stimulation. Make the socialization process an exciting and fun experience for your Pomsky.

# Introducing Your Pomsky to People

" *My Pomsky Cammi took on more of the Husky side of the genetics, so she is very hyper and needs a lot of exercise. She is also very, very welcoming to strangers. She would gladly go up to a complete stranger and walk off with them if I let her! (This could also be a positive that they are so friendly, depends what you want in a dog. Not a good guard dog, that's for sure!)"*

**Shannon Vander Weide**

*Photo: Sheron Steele – Ashoka Ariel*

Other than raising a Pomsky that is good around other dogs or other animals, you will want to raise a Pomsky that is also good around people that are outside of his family or his pack. This will also take time and patience for you and your Pomsky.

It may be surprising to many that dogs can be nervous around people of all sorts of ages, races, genders, sizes, style of clothing, and etc. Although, it may sound silly, you will want to socialize and introduce your dog to a lot of different people and different types of people. A dog can notice a lot more than you think. For example, if never socialized with men, and only raised by a woman, a dog, upon meeting a man, can become anxious or nervous. Alternatively, a dog may be nervous around a person who walks with a cane or wears glasses or a large hat. However small or silly the detail may seem, a dog can and will notice it and it may make him nervous or anxious.

To help this, you will want to expose your dog to a myriad of different people. Again, you want to reward and good and positive reactions and behaviors that your dog exhibits. You do not want to reward any fearful behavior that he may show.

Keep the interactions short. You will want to also start by introducing your puppy to people that you trust before you start to walk out and about, exposing your Pomsky pup to all sorts of people. You will want to also keep a keen eye on your dog and his body language. If you notice him getting anxious or threatened, you will want to be sure to give him the breaks that he needs.

Socializing your dogs with people is also important to raising a happy, healthy, and confident dog. You want to make these experiences relaxed, calm, and fun for your dog. Your dog feeds off of your energy. If you compose yourself in a calm and confident manner, your dog will feed off of this energy. When working with people you trust to begin with, you begin to build a strong foundation for your dog as he learns to trust people.

# Introducing Your Pomsky to Children

Children need to learn proper ways to interact with dogs. However, at the same time, you also need to help your dog become more comfortable with children through socialization. Children can sometimes be scary to dogs. Children are unpredictable, loud, and can sometimes be rough to the dog.

Breed specific, some Pomskies tend to do well with children. However, it is mostly dependent up what the Pomsky inherits from the Pomeranian father or Siberian Husky mother. Siberian Huskies tend to be great around children. Pomeranians, on the other hand, are normally nervous around children. Pomskies can actually inherit either trait. Consistent and early socialization can help your Pomsky to become more comfortable with children and not be as nervous around younger children.

You will want to start by working with children that are polite and respectful of dogs. You also need to keep the time interacting with the children short to start. You want to avoid overwhelming your puppy.

When meeting a young puppy, children can become very excited and sometimes too much excitement can be frightening for a young Pomsky. Help to teach the children about patience and respecting your puppy's space. The children should know to listen to you, or another trusted adult, about when it is time to leave a dog along. A child needs to learn proper respect of the dog and how to pet and carefully handle a dog.

Interacting with dogs can be a great learning experience for children. Dogs, when properly socialized, can demonstrate great love and loyalty to their smaller human pack members. Dogs are powerful animals that can only communicate through body language. With that said, it is important to remember this when children are around the new puppy.

Encourage the children that are interacting with your puppy to begin to read your Pomsky's body language. The dog should be allowed to come to the child calmly. You are ultimately in charge of your dog. You also need to understand that it is okay to stop the interaction if something is not working. If you notice your dog is becoming increasingly nervous around the children, you need to stop the interaction. Your puppy trusts you. You should respect that trust by not forcing him into something that makes him nervous, scared, or tense. Provide your Pomsky with a lot of treats and positive reinforcement for your dog to make the experience a positive one for him.

Children can be scary for a young dog, including your Pomsky. Learning how to interact and respect a dog is important for a child. Interactions need to be kept short and sweet. A lot of positive reinforcement throughout the interactions can help to make these experiences positive ones.

# CHAPTER 9

# Training Your Pomsky

" *A huge positive of the Pomsky breed would be how smart this breed is! They are very quick learners, which make them a great family pet. They are very loyal to their family and the kids in the family."*

*Makala Braun*

Photo: Makala Braun

## Be Firm and Be Consistent

When training your Pomsky, firm tones and consistency in your demands, expectations, and rewards is vital to properly training your Pomsky. The Pomeranian side of your Pomsky is very intelligent but can also be very stubborn.

You will also need to be assertive and have strong leadership skills in order to run successful training sessions. You want your Pomsky to listen to you. He is less apt to listen to you if he feels as though he is more in charge than you. A Pomsky that has inherited his Pomeranian father's stubbornness runs the risk of suffering from small dog syndrome.

In order to maintain consistency during training, you will want to hold daily training sessions. You also will want to avoid leaving your puppy alone for long periods of time. You want your puppy to trust you, especially if you want him to listen to you and obey your commands. A Pomsky puppy that feels he has to fend for himself and that does not form that bond with his owner is more likely to develop small dog syndrome and refuse to listen to you.

All in all, if you train your puppy with consistent, firm, and kind training methods, you are setting your Pomsky up for success. By being firm, consistent, and kind to your Pomsky, you will quickly gain his trust. You will want the training sessions to be short and fun. If your Pomsky sees learning commands as fun and entertaining and rewarding for him, he is more likely to be an obedient Puppy. You can break up the training sessions with play time as a reward for his hard work. This will make your Pomsky see the training as play, and not boring work that will force him to lose his focus.

# Operant Conditioning

Almost all dogs respond well to reward based training. The science behind this success is most commonly known as **operant conditioning**. When puppies are trained with treats and rewards and positive reinforcement, the behaviors are more likely to be repeated. Negative reinforcement can really only lead to a dog that is fearful of you. You want your Pomsky to trust you as his owner. You do not want him to be fearful of you in any way. Trust is foundation of the relationship between you and your Pomsky.

Operant conditioning, as defined by the dictionary, is learning that is controlled by the outcome. In other words, as a new dog owner and new dog trainer, as your new Pomsky performs the desired behaviors you request of him, you praise him and reward him with affection and treats. The theory behind operant conditioning is then that your puppy will repeat these desired behaviors as he comes to realize that when he performs the commands that are asked of him, he is rewarded greatly. The learning is then controlled by the outcome. The outcome is that he will be rewarded and the learning is the fact that he soon discovers that in order to receive that reward, he has to first listen to his master by sitting, laying down, heeling, or using the bathroom in the designated area.

# Rewards

Again, the most effective form of training for your Pomsky is reward based training. Your Pomsky learns best what is expected of him by when he is rewarded for doing something that pleases you or for doing something that is expected of him, such as asking to go to the bathroom or waiting calmly at the door before going for a walk.

There are many different ways to reward your Pomsky puppy for a job well done. Many trainers start out with treats, but in fact, rewarding your Pomsky can include a wide range of actions. Different types of rewards can include verbal praise, giving your Pomsky extra attention, playing with your Pomsky, and the standard of giving your Pomsky food treats.

If you are planning on giving your Pomsky treats for his reward, as many trainers do to start out, you will want to find treats that are healthy for your Pomsky puppy along with something that he likes. Eventually, you will want to wean out the treats and reward your Pomsky more with verbal praise over food rewards.

The timing of when you reward your dog is so important to properly train your Pomsky. You will want to reward your dog as soon as he performs the desired command when you ask him to. Praise or an immediate treat along with verbal praise is essential to successfully train your Pomsky. If you praise and reward your Pomsky too early, he will not fully understand what he did exactly to earn the reward. If you praise and reward your Pomsky too late after the desired behavior he will not make the correlation between the action he did well and the reason why he is getting the reward.

Also, while training, you will want to avoid letting your Pomsky puppy see the treats until after he complies with what you are asking of him. If he sees the treat before he performs the action, he is more listening to the treat and not the command you have given him. In other words, he is only comply with what you are asking of him because he sees the treat and not because you asked him to do something.

Your Pomsky, along with most other dogs, respond extremely well to reward based training. These rewards can be verbal praise, affection, play, or food. You need to time the rewards perfectly in order for the reward based training to be successful. You also want your Pomsky to listen to what you are telling him and to comply to your commands when you tell him, not when he sees a treat and knows that a treat is coming his way. In order to do this, you want to keep the treat out of his field of vision. Only show him the treat when he has completely com-plied with your command. This can help you and your Pomsky to build a strong bond based on loyalty, trust, and respect.

# Be Patient

With the great intelligence that comes with a Pomsky, there also comes great stubbornness. You will need to be patient, calm, but still assertive with your Pomsky. If you are not patient, calm, and assertive with your Pomsky, your young puppy could end up showing symptoms of **small dog syndrome** or other behav-ioral issues.

All puppies have short attention spans. To help with this, you need to give your Pomskies short training sessions mixed in with play time and positive rein-forcement. Sessions should only be ten to fifteen minutes long. You can do sev-eral training sessions a day when they are short and sweet for your Pomsky. After each training session, you can reward your Pomsky with play time or treats.

You can train your Pomsky pup in any room or anywhere and at any time. You want to keep your Pomsky guessing and expect to listen to you. If you keep the training sessions in only one place, you set yourself up to not be listened to by your Pomsky. By only focusing on training in the home, for example, your Pomsky may end up learning that the only time that he needs to listen to you is while you are in the home.

You also want to practice patience with your puppy because many of the commands will have to be repeated for long spans of time. A Pomsky, or any oth-er dog, will not necessarily master the command of sit, for example, on the first try, let alone in the first session. This is why consistency is so important. You need to practice a specific command in the same way each session until he under-stands what is expected of him and begins to comply with what you ask of him dependably.

Patience is important when working with your Pomsky to train him. Your puppy has a very short attention span and many of the commands will need to be repeated a lot. He will also not completely understand what you are asking of him immediately. In order to help your Pomsky be successful in his training, there will need to be a lot of repetition, praise, and reward. If you can remain calm and sup-portive of your Pomsky, you can work to raise and train a dog that is happy and confident in himself and a dog that can trust you and love you unconditionally.

# CHAPTER 10

# Basic Commands

## Overview

Training your Pomsky can create a bond between human and animal that is unbreakable. You have to help your Pomsky to understand that you are the leader of your puppy's pack.

To aid in your training, you should carry yourself confidently. Your puppy feeds off of your body language. If you feel confident and are exuding that confidence while training your Pomsky, your Pomsky puppy will know that you are in charge. He will be more likely to listen to you more readily. You need to know the energy that you are feeding your Pomsky. You want to let him know that you are in charge.

You want to know your puppy's limits. If you begin to notice that your Pomsky is losing focus and beginning to run away, your Pomsky has become overstimulated. Once overstimulated, you need to give your Pomsky a break. You want to give your Pomsky a break before he takes one himself. You need to set the schedule with your Pomsky, not him. When you are in charge of the training sessions, and maintain control over when the training starts and stops, you continue to maintain control over your Pomsky and the training. This will help to prevent your Pomsky from becoming stubborn and not wanting to listen to you.

Again, patience is important while training your Pomsky. You want to maintain a calm and assertive demeanor in front of your Pomsky pup. If you do not demonstrate confidence or assertiveness in front of your new puppy, he may not see you as an authority figure and is less likely to listen to you.

This chapter focuses on some basic commands that you can teach your Pomsky. It each skill is important to teach your Pomsky in its own way. Success in teaching your Pomsky these commands can help to create a happy, confident, and polite Pomsky.

# Sit

Sit is a great basic command to teach your Pomsky. This command is a basic foundation for many other commands that you will teach your Pomsky to obey. Remember, during training, to maintain confident in yourself and this will guide your Pomsky to realize that you are in charge.

To start, stand in front of your dog. Have a treat in your hand, pinched between your fingers. Hold the treat just in front of your dog's nose, so he can smell it. Then, move the treat slowly above your puppy's head. Instruct your Pomsky to sit by giving the command "Sit" as you move the treat. Your Pomsky should begin to tilt his head back to follow the treat. When he cannot see it any more you should encourage your puppy to sit in order to continue to watch the treat. As soon as he sits, you will want to give him praise immediately followed by giving him his reward. Right now,

Photo: Makala Braun

that reward is the treat. You will need to repeat this command with this method multiple times. You want to be consistent. You want to say the command in the same tone of voice as well as have the same body language and hand gestures. Your dog can actually better understand your body language and tone of voice versus what you are actually saying.

Slowly, you will want to begin to remove the treat from the training. You want your Pomsky to listen to you because you are the leader of his pack. You do not want your Pomsky to listen to you only because you are holding a treat in your hand.

Once your Pomsky seems to be getting the hang of sitting with the treat, take away the treat. Try this by hiding the treat in your other hand. Instruct your Pomsky to sit. You need to use the same hand you did before when telling your Pomsky to sit. This keeps the tone and command the same, as well as the movement. The only difference between each exercise is that you will now be giving your Pomsky his reward from the other hand immediately after he complies with the command properly. This keeps it consistent with your Pomsky as well as making it more challenging for him. He is beginning to learn to listen to your body language and tone of voice, rather than the actual treat.

After you phase out the treat from being in your hand, you can start to fade out your hand signal. Try this after your Pomsky is consistently sitting with only seeing your hand movement and hearing you say "sit." Eventually you can tell him to sit without any hand movements. If he complies right away, you need to praise him immediately and reward him with the treat that you have in your other hand, again. If he does not comply right away, you may need to repeat the command with the hand motion. Keep repeating this exercise until your Pomsky pup has mastered the command sit.

You can begin to make it more difficult by increasing the wait time for receiving the treat. Always praise your dog right away, but maybe you can hold off on giving your Pomsky the treat immediately. This will help to prevent your puppy from becoming reliant on the treat.

Some owners and trainers like to teach sit for the dog to greet any guests that may come to the house and any new people they may come across. You will want to have your dog sit before the excitement of the new friend becomes too much for him. As soon as he does and is exhibiting calm behavior, praise and reward your Pomsky immediately. You will also want to continue to praise and reward your Pomsky as the puppy continues to hold the sitting position. You will also want to repeat this. You can ask friends to come over and practice this skill with your Pomsky.

# Stay

Stay is a great command to teach your Pomsky, especially if you want him to not follow you somewhere or remain in a part of the house while you get something or for any other number of reasons. This is a command that should be taught after your Pomsky has begun to master "Sit" to an extent. If your Pomsky knows to lie down it can also be helpful while training.

Photo: Makala Braun

You should start by commanding your Pomsky to sit or lie down. Before rewarding him, command him to "stay." Begin by counting to a smaller number. Count to ten to start.

As he holds the "stay," praise him and reward him with a treat. You will first have to release your dog with another command word such as "okay" and then reward your Pomsky and praise him.

You will need to repeat this exercise multiple times with your Pomsky. Once he begins to master the command "stay," increase the difficulty. As you have your Pomsky stay, increase the time that he has to remain before releasing him and then praising and rewarding your Pomsky. As you increase the time, begin increasing the distance between you and your Pomsky. Start by having your Pomsky "stay." Then slowly move backward. If your dog moves before you give the release command, bring him back to the spot where you started and try again.

As you begin to be successful in the training, you can begin to add things to keep your puppy occupied during the time he is expected to stay. You can bring him toys or his favorite bed or his favorite chew things.

Again, you will need to keep your sessions short and consistent. This will help to set up your Pomsky for success and keep him from becoming bored during the sessions.

## Lay Down

The best time to teach your Pomsky to lie down is after the sit command has started to become mastered. First have your Pomsky sit. Then tell your Pomsky to "lay down" or give the command "down." Pick one command and keep it the same throughout all training.

Arm yourself with plenty of treats. Hold a treat in front of your Pomsky's nose as you give him the command. Then move the treat down to the floor slowly, placing it between your puppy's paws. Allow the dog to smell and taste the treat, but not eat it. Have your Pomsky follow the treat with his nose. Then once the treat gets to the floor, move the treat along the floor, making an "L" motion.

*Photo: Makala Braun*

You are essentially luring your dog into a laying down position. As soon as he is successful in his attempt praise him and reward him with the treat. Have your dog stand and do it again.

This method does not always work the smoothest and you may need to do some trouble shooting. You can first try using treats that you know will lure and attract your dog.

Sometimes, your Pomsky puppy may want to stand to get to the treat. If he does this, quickly take away the treat and try again. You can also try sitting on the floor in front of your puppy. Have your legs straight out in front of you with the dog sitting on the left or right side of you. You should then bend your knees up to make a tent shape. Then, you will want to try the same luring "L" motion with the treat. Continue dragging the treat along the floor and under your legs. As soon as your puppy lays down to get to the treat, praise him excitedly and give him the treat.

Keep practicing the exercise every day. You should keep the sessions short and reward successful and even non-successful training sessions with play time at the end. You want your puppy to think that the training can be fun, not a chore or boring. If he has fun doing it, he will look forward to these training sessions.

Similarly to when you started teaching your Pomsky to sit, you will want to fade out the lure and begin only using your hand while you say the cue word. You want to keep your words consistent as well as the tone and hand signals. Then fade out the hand signal to have your Pomsky rely solely on your voice command.

Keep practicing this exercise and begin adding distractions as your puppy begins to more frequently perform the desired action. The distraction will help challenge your puppy and condition him to listen to you in real life situations when you are both surrounded by distractions.

# Come

There are a couple methods used to teach your dog to come to you. This command is vital when you and your puppy are traveling out and about, to visits to the dog park, if your puppy gets loose (God forbid), or a number of other reasons.

Photo: Makala Braun

You can start by having your puppy on a leash. Tell him "come" and take a step back. Keep stepping back until your Pomsky follows you. Reward and praise him as soon as he catches up to you. Keep practicing this until he does not need you to back off before following your command.

Another method to teach your Pomsky to come to you when called requires a longer training leash and a helper. Using the longer training leash, have someone helping you by holding the dog as you begin to move away. After you are a certain distance away, turn and call your dog's name and say "Come" in an excited tone. This tone will help to get your puppy to want to come to you. When he comes to you, praise him and reward him with treats.

As you continue these training sessions, begin adding space between you and your puppy. You can try this exercise in the house, in different rooms, or outside in the yard. You do not want to do this exercise out in the open until you are confident that your dog will come to you immediately when he is called. You can begin adding distractions, making the practice session more like a real life event. You can call your Pomsky by name, followed by the command word. When your Pomsky comes, reward him with a favorite treat of his.

"Come" is a very important command that you will want your Pomsky to master. Having a dog that will reliably come to you when called, regardless of what he is distracted by can mean the difference between a dog that respects you and a dog that does not see you as his alpha. Remember to keep training sessions short and fun for your puppy to keep him focused and make it so he wants to come to you when he is called.

# Off

You will want to use the command "off" for when you want to get your dog off of you or off of the furniture. The command "down" is most commonly used when asking a down to lay down or lay down in his dog bed. The "off" command is more for when you want your dog to get off of something or someone.

You can start practicing this concept with your Pomsky by having your dog's front paws on your lap or on a box. Normally, using your lap is easier. When you give the command "off" use a firm, not mean, tone. If your dog complies, praise him and give him a reward. If he does not listen to the command, you can stand slowly as you repeat the command at the same time.

Practice this command regularly. When your dog is on the furniture and you do not want him to be, tell him "off" while pointing at the ground. Initially, while first learning it, he may need some help. Praise your Pomsky and give him treats when he follows your command.

# Give/Drop

This command is best taught using a bargaining method on top of the positive reinforcement that you have been practicing with the other commands. Puppies are curious and can easily get ahold of something they should not. Teaching your puppy to drop something or give it back can be very important and helpful for future shenanigans your puppy may get into.

Photo: Lexi Wo

preciouspomskies.com

When your Pomsky gets a hold of something that you want him to drop, be sure to first have things that are more attractive to him than what he has in his mouth on hand. Tell him "give" or "drop." You should keep the command word consistent as with the other commands you are teaching your Pomsky.

As you give the command, offer your puppy the new treat or toy in exchange. When he drops it, reward him with praise and the treat. If he does not drop the item in his mouth, you may want to try another more appealing treat.

# Leave it

The command "leave it" teaches dogs to leave something, which you do not want them to be touching, alone. It can be a great command, much like "give" or "drop" to teach a puppy for behavioral reasons.

First things first, you need to look for the behavior that you want him to perform. You need to do this by luring him into the behavior. Start by sitting with your dog, holding a treat in your hand. Hold the hand out to your dog with a closed fist so he cannot get to it and tell him "leave it." He will want to get to the treat. He may bark, paw, or lick at your hand, but you want to ignore this behavior and not respond to it. Wait until he stops.

As soon as he stops, praise him and give him the treat. You want to continue repeating this exercise until he moves away immediately following the command. Give the treat from your other hand. This training may take a couple of days to begin mastery or just one session. It really just depends on the dog.

You can try challenging him in different ways. You can try by increasing the wait time before giving your Pomsky the treat, so he has to leave the item for longer amounts of time.

You can also make it more of a challenge by moving the location. You can try putting the treat on the floor. Have a piece of food, maybe something like kibble, on the floor and something tastier as a reward for the dog leaving it. This type of training can be hard at times. Some dogs are aggressive with their food. The training for this commands must be completed with caution. You may need to seek professional help, especially as a beginning dog owner, for a dog that is showing any kind of food aggression.

You can practice this command anywhere. You will want to keep tasty treats with you at all times when you are with your dog so you can capitalize on many learning opportunities.

# Walk

Walking on a leash is not an instinct that is born to puppies. When first putting your Pomsky on a leash, you will notice that your new puppy is not yet able to properly walk on a leash. He does not know how to yet. You will have to teach him to do this.

Before working on walking on the leash, you will want to tire out your Pomsky, especially when first starting out. This will help to lessen the amount your Pomsky pulls during training sessions. When training to walk on a leash you will need to provide your puppy

*Photo: Sheron Steele - Ashoka*

with a lot of treats and positive reinforcement. You also want to walk fast during the walks. This aids in avoiding your puppy from getting a new smell and becoming distracted on the walk.

You also need to make sure your puppy is calm before you go on the walk. If he is too excited prior to the walk, that over excitement will carry over into the walk making it unproductive in training.

During walks you can work on teaching your puppy how to heel. However, you will want to start training for this command in a stationary position as to not confuse your puppy to start off. The proper positioning of a dog that is heeling is that his feet cannot be past your feet. You will reward your puppy with a treat each time he is in the right position. You can actually use the treat to guide the dog around into the right position and then have him sit in the heel position.

Once your puppy is able to do this in a stationary position, you can begin to add movement. You want your puppy to be standing behind you, not ahead of you. The ultimate goal of the heel command is to have your dog walking with you. When using heel while moving, you can introduce the leash. However, you do not want to use the leash to teach the dog to heel. The leash is only there to redirect other walking manners. To practice heel with you puppy while walking, you will continue to use the lure method for the puppy. This maintains uniformity, helping your puppy to succeed in the training.

To start, you want to have the sessions be short. To increase the challenge for your dog, increase the amount of time that you want your dog to remain in heel. Reward your puppy the longer he stays in heel. Keep in mind that you only want to praise and reward your puppy when he is in the right position. That way he knows what he is doing right.

Having a dog that can properly walk and heel while on the leash is important. You want to raise a dog that you can feel comfortable and confident walking out in your neighborhood.

# What Comes Next?

After your dog has been trained in these basic skills and commands, you may want to look to train your puppy to perform other commands and tricks. You may want to train your dog to do simple tricks like paw or shake.

Beyond that, however, there is no limit to what you can train your Pomsky to do. Dogs are intelligent animals and really just want to please you. Your dog will see you as his alpha and will respect you, love you, and be the most loyal friend you can have.

Training your dog is a great way to build this connection between you and him. Many people train their dogs for dog shows or athletic events. You may want to train your dog to fetch, play Frisbee, and get you a drink from the fridge, or something as simple as barking on command.

The point is the sky is the limit for what you and your dog can accomplish. You want to make these trainings to be fun and like a game. Training can be stressful, but you have to show tenacity, patience, and calm. Your dog feeds off of your energy and if you are having fun training your dog, your dog will have fun training with you. You can make it a game and you and your puppy can accomplish anything!

# CHAPTER 11

## Nutrition

## What Can I Feed My Pomsky?

A proper diet is essential to raising a happy and healthy Pomksy. Many dog foods specialize in healthy diets, healthy coats, or giving your dog the energy that he needs. You want to find food that is a high quality variety of dry kibble.

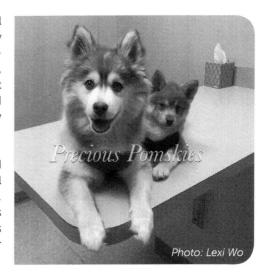
Photo: Lexi Wo

The dog food that you feed your Pomsky needs to meet all of your puppy's nutritional needs. Pomskies are high energy dogs and need the proper food that has the proper nutrients to fuel their highly energetic bodies.

If you are unsure as to what brand or kind of dog food that you want to feed your Pomsky, do not hesitate to ask your veterinarian or the breeder. The veterinarian and breeders of Pomskies are highly education on the kinds of foods that are good for your puppy.

## Puppy Food vs. People Food

As discussed earlier, there are a lot of foods that are good for people that are not good for your dog. Many of these foods are actually very dangerous for your precious puppy to consume. One example is grapes. Dogs are unable to digest and metabolize grapes.

On the other hand, some human foods are safe for your dog to eat. These foods should be fed minimally. You always should check with your veterinarian about what "people foods" are okay for your puppy to eat.

Some human foods that are alright for your Pomsky to consume are listed below:

- Garlic is a human food that can actually be beneficial for your dog in small portions.

- Lean meat is okay for your dog as well. Usually lean meat is white meat from chicken as well as from turkey. Lean meats are good to use as treats and they provide good protein. You can give these lean meats to your dog raw or cooked.

- Raw eggs and cooked eggs are also a good source of protein and vitamins for your dog.

- Some fruits are alright for your dog to eat. Such fruits are bananas, apple slices, strawberries, blueberries, and watermelon. Be sure to remove the seeds, especially since apple seeds are poisonous to dogs. These fruits, however, are great to use as treats and to help with training. The fruits can also help to cool down your dog on a hot day.

- Vegetables like carrots, green beans, cucumber slices, and zucchini slices all make great treats and rewards for your dog.

- Plain baked potatoes are alright for your dog to eat. However, it is not the best. If you plan on feeding your dog a baked potato, it cannot have any toppings.

- White rice and white pasta is also okay for a dog to eat. They are usually used for a dog with an upset stomach, especially when combined with boiled white chicken. This type of meal helps to nourish a dog having issues getting nourishment because the dog is sick.

So, while there are a few human foods that are safe for dogs to consume, you will want to do so with caution. Dogs' digestive systems are different from ours. Food that we can digest easily cannot always be easily digested by your loving pooch.

# CHAPTER 12

## Grooming

### Understanding Your Pomsky's Coat

Pomskies, with their Siberian Husky and Pomeranian heritage, are heavy shedders. They require a lot of grooming because of their thick coats. Before knowing what to do with the coats for grooming, you have to become familiar with the coats and understand how they work.

Pomskies have a **Double Layered** coat. It is a soft an fluffy coat that sheds a lot. There is an **outer layer** that can be fluffy like the Pomsky's Pomeranian father or sleek and smooth like the Pomsky's Siberian Husky mother. The **undercoat** or **inner coat** sheds quickly. It is denser and only slightly different in length between each dog. Most Pomskies' coats are much like their Siberian Husky parents and are only low to medium shedders. Brushing their fur regularly will help to control the shedding.

The Pomsky's double coat is good for colder climates. They need to be brushed regularly to also keep the coat healthy. They should be brushed once or twice a week at the very least. Sometimes quick daily brushings are helpful to keep the coat healthy and shiny. Brushing removes dead hairs and tangles. Every day brushing is not always necessary and is mostly done for looks.

You can use the times that you are grooming your Pomsky to calm him. These grooming times can be used to get your Pomsky puppy used to someone touching sensitive areas such as his paws, ears, and tail.

### Bathing Routines

Bathing your dog is important, however it is not something that needs to be done on a consistent basis. In fact, you only want to bath your Pomsky when completely necessary. You really only need to give your Pomsky a bath one to two baths a moth. You only want to use gentle shampoo. Doggy shampoo and clean water is the best. You do not need any more products to care for the Pomsky's fur as the fur can take care of itself for the most part.

# Nail Trimming

Trimmed nails is an important part to keeping your Pomsky properly groomed. Regular filing can be done to keep the nails from becoming too sharp. Regular nail care can also help with prevention of nail infections.

# Brushing Teeth

Pomeranians tend to have many dental health issues. These issues can easily be passed on to your Pomsky pup. Proper dental health care, for this reason, is very important. Your Pomsky will need annual dental cleaning done by a professional. Your veterinarian can also do this for you. If not, he or she will probably be able to refer you to a number of places that can do this for you.

# Hair Cuts

Because of your Pomsky's special fur, you will want to avoid cutting the fur. The undercoat actually protects your fuzzy puppy from the heat as well as the cold. Cutting your Pomskies fur can actually be hazardous to his health overall.

# CHAPTER 13

# Basic Health Care

## Fleas and Ticks

Fleas and ticks are **parasites** that are common with any mammal. These parasites can cause many different illnesses. It is vital that you protect your pet against fleas and ticks. Getting sick from a tick or flea, without the proper vaccinations can lead to many illnesses. Many of these illnesses can actually be deadly to your puppy. Therefore, proper precautions must be made to protect your Pomsky.

Photo: Makala Braun

Fleas are wingless insects. They are very small insects that can jump surprisingly far for their small size. These fleas are normally found on dogs, cats, opossums, coyotes, raccoons, and foxes. They are not found on all mammals. They like to burrow and hide in the fur of the fore mentioned animals. Fleas feed off the blood of the host. They can spread diseases like bartonellosis and tapeworm.

Ticks are **arachnids**. They are much like spiders. These parasites are found on a large number more animals than fleas. Ticks are normally found on birds, rodents, snakes, lizards, foxes, deer, squirrels, rabbits, opossums, raccoons, cattle, cats, dogs, and humans. Ticks, much like fleas, also feed off the blood of the host. Ticks are much sturdier than fleas and can easily survive cold temperatures. Ticks can spread diseases that can prove fatal for your dog. The diseases spread by these ticks are lyme disease and Rocky Mountain Spotted Fever.

Your veterinarian will, during annual check-ups, give your dog vaccinations to help defend against many of the diseases spread by these parasites. However, proper protection must also be done by you, the dog owner and care taker. There are many brands of medication that are prescribed by your veterinarian to protect your dog from fleas and ticks. Normally these are given to your pet orally or spread, in liquid form, between the shoulder blades of your dog once every month.

# Worms

Normally, dogs can have a strong enough immune system to kill many illnesses as well as certain parasites that can cause such illnesses. Dogs can sometimes kill off parasites such as worms with their strong immune systems, however, many times your dog may need help from a veterinarian.

Worms are a parasite that develop, usually, when a dog is nutrient deficient. This is normally domesticated dogs that have this issue versus wolves or other canines that are born and raised in the wild. The natural diet of a canine is meat and bones. Domesticated dogs do not get as much meat or bones in their diets. Most dog food companies tend to substitute the meat and bone diet with corn, rice, and chicken meal among other filler ingredients. These fillers, for the most part, are pretty unhealthy for your dog. The lack of meat and bones in the dogs' diets causes a deficiency in some nutrients. This lack of proper nutrition is very tough on the dog's immune system. This makes it difficult for the dogs to fight off illnesses such as worms and other parasites.

There are five common worms found that plague our dogs. There are different symptoms for the different worms as well. If you are finding that your dog is showing any of the below mentioned symptoms, you will need to take precautions immediately, including taking your puppy to the veterinarian.

The tapeworm is one of the five worms that are commonly found in the dogs. This type of worm is normally found on the inner lining of the intestinal wall. The young worms, normally the eggs, are passed through the dog's feces. Tapeworms drain the nutrition from the dog it is infecting.

The roundworms and the hookworms are the most common type of worms found in dogs. These worms are normally found in the stomach and intestinal walls of the dogs.

Heartworms are another common worm that infect dogs and make them sick. Heartworms live in the blood vessels of the dogs. These worms can cause blockages and actually be fatal to your dog. Heartworms can be spread by mosquitos and other blood drinking insects. Heartworms are very difficult to detect. Unfortunately, once heartworms are detected, the damage has already been done to the dog.

Whipworms are a final type of common worms found in dogs. These worms are usually found attached to the walls of the small intestines and large intestines. Whipworms are also hard to detect. This type of worm does not reproduce as quickly as the other worms. However, the scary thing about this type of worm is that the eggs, once laid, can live up to five years without hatching. They will wait that long without hatching until the whipworm eggs can attach to a host.

There is a wide range of symptoms that can cue in a dog owner to a worm infestation. One of these symptoms is coughing. A lot of worms can cause coughing. Heartworms, when at a high infestation level, can cause coughing. Hookworms and roundworms can also cause your dog to cough.

Vomiting is also another symptom. Vomiting is normally caused by worms in the stomach. The worms in the stomach can make a dog's stomach very uneasy. In some cases, the worms can be found in the bile.

Diarrhea is a symptom of worms that are most often found in the intestines of the dogs. The worms that cause diarrhea and are attached to the intestines can easily steal the nutrients from the dog. The worms then lay the eggs in the intestines and the eggs are then found in the feces and can be spread to other dogs.

If your dog is displaying a lot of low energy, you will want to get him checked out by your veterinarian. Low energy can normally be caused by worms that stay in the heart. These worms can make it difficult for the dog's blood to circulate the oxygen properly as well as circulate the nutrients it needs to. These worms that cause low energy also take up the nutrients that the dog needs for himself.

You may notice a lot of puppies, when they are first born, tend to have a little pot belly. This is due to the fact that a lot of puppies are born with worms already in them. Some worms are actually passed on from a mother to her puppies during pregnancy. This causes the puppies to have a pot belly. However, the little pot belly is not only seen puppies. Many adult dogs can show signs of a pot belly because of a worm infestation.

If you notice your dog losing a significant amount of weight, you will want to take him to the veterinarian as soon as possible. Worms tend to take any nutrition that your dog desperately needs. These worms may actually absorb any food that the dog it is infesting may ingest.

A dull coat can also be a symptom of a worm infestation. You may notice your dog's coat is becoming spotty and start to lose its shine. You may also notice, on your dog's skin, rashes forming.

An itchy dog can also be a red flag to a dog that is infested with worms. There are worms that can actually infect parts of the dog's skin and thus making the dog feel itchy. If you notice your dog continually scratching a specific area, you may want to treat your dog for worms.

Dogs, when infected by worms that are found in or around the rectum, can cause them to scoot across the floor. This type of infection can be very painful for your dog. The dog scooting across the floor is a way that he will try to remove this irritation. While it can be alarming, a dog scooting across the ground is not always due to a worm infestation. However, that does not mean you should not look into the reasoning behind the scooting behavior, just to be sure you are covering your bases.

Finally, worm infested feces are a sure sign of your dog being infested with worms. Many worms lay their eggs in the small and large intestines. The eggs are easy to spot in the fecal matter. However, it is also easy to transfer these kinds of worms to other dogs because of this.

Worms are a nuisance to have your dogs infested by. Veterinarians, during the initial check-up and future check-ups will test and treat your dog for worms. He will also suggest necessary medication to help to prevent different worms, usually heartworms.

Even if treated as a preventative measure, you will want to keep an eye out for any of the symptoms mentioned above. Parasites like worms can be very hazardous to your Pomsky's health. The health of your dog will be one of your top priorities, right there with his happiness. One of the best ways to keep your dog happy is to keep your dog healthy.

# Finding a Veterinarian

Finding a veterinarian that you can trust is one of the most important things to do before bringing home your Pomsky. A veterinarian is someone who will care for your dog when he is too sick for you to care for yourself. A veterinarian is well versed in animal health and you should never feel hesitant to take your dog to the veterinarian if you notice anything strange in his physical appearance or behavior. Some symptoms can be signs to a less significant disease or a life threatening disease.

With that said, you will want to find a veterinarian that you feel comfortable going to. You do not want to go to a veterinarian that you cannot trust with your dog. As you will quickly begin to realize, your sweet Pomsky puppy will quickly tug on your heartstrings. Therefore, you will want a veterinarian that you know will take good care of you beloved pooch. There are a lot of qualities that are the makings of a great pet.

First off, you will want a veterinarian that can run a good practice. This includes a practice that has great customer service. You want to walk into the veterinarian's office and know that your dog will be taken care of. If the veterinarian office that you walk into feels unorganized, unwelcoming, chaotic, or other disconcerting signs, you may not want to take your pet to this office. If the office makes you feel uncomfortable, your pet will feel uncomfortable. Find an office that you feel happy, comfortable, and confident to take your pet to. Along those lines, you want a veterinarian that has good time management skill. You want a veterinarian that easily keeps his appointment times and moves them along quickly without compromising the quality of service that he provides.

You also want to have a veterinarian that communicates easily with you. There is a lot of medical information that is passed on to you about your pet. You may want a veterinarian that can describe and explain to you everything that he needs to in a manner that is easily understandable.

A compassionate veterinarian is an awesome veterinarian to take you precious Pomsky to. You want a veterinarian that truly cares for his job, what he does, and the pets that he cares for. You want a veterinarian that is also passionate about what he or she does. Along the same lines, you want a veterinarian that is dedicated to his job. You want a veterinarian that will not easily give up. You want a veterinarian that you know will be there for you and your pet and someone that you can really rely on.

As obvious as it seems, you want a veterinarian that is able to handle animals of various shapes and sizes. You want a veterinarian that is also knowledgeable. A proper veterinarian should be able to be confidently handle your dog, regardless of his size. A proper veterinarian should also know what could be ailing your dog as well as how to take care of any issues that arise.

Finally, it would be beneficial for you to find a veterinarian that is able to make quick decisions. This does not mean that the veterinarian should be making rash decisions. There are times that a veterinarian will have to make quick decisions, especially in emergency situations. You want a veterinarian who, when under pressure, can make well thought out decisions in a pinch. These quick decision making skills can end up saving your dog's life someday.

While all of these qualities are great for helping you to decide on a veterinarian, the most important quality is that you feel comfortable with the veterinarian you choose in the end. He or she is someone that you can talk to easily and ask questions. If you get your Pomsky from a local breeder, you can ask your breeder about veterinarians that they trust if you are having trouble finding a reputable veterinarian.

# Vaccines

Vaccines are issued to keep your dog from catching many different disease. Your veterinarian can tell you what ones are best for your puppy.

There are certain vaccines that are required, others that are recommended, and others that are really only recommended depending on where you live. In 2006, the American Animal Hospital Association's Canine Task Force revised the guidelines of core, non-core, and not recommended vaccines for dogs.

Core vaccines are vaccines that are important for all dogs to have. These vaccines are canine parvovirus, distemper, canine hepatitis, and rabies. Non-core vaccines are vaccines are suggested based on if the dog is at risk or not. Non-core vaccines protect against diseases such as Bordetella bronchiseptica, borrelia, burgdoferi, and leptospira bacteria.

Your vet will know what to give your Pomsky and when your Pomsky should be vaccinated for a disease.

Most dogs should not show a negative side effect after being injected with some of the vaccines. However, sometimes an adverse reaction can happen. Some symptoms that you will want to watch for after a vaccine are fever, sluggishness, loss of appetite, facial swelling or hives, vomiting, diarrhea, pain, swelling, redness, or loss of hair around where the vaccine was injected, lameness, collapsing, hard time breathing, or seizures. If you notice any of these symptoms you will want to contact your veterinarian.

All in all, vaccinations are important for your Pomsky to keep him safe from a wide range of diseases. If not vaccinated, these illnesses can make your Pomsky very sick and in many cases can result in an untimely death. Again, your goal in raising a Pomsky is to raise a puppy into a happy and healthy dog.

# Keeping Your Pomsky Healthy

Overall, the Pomsky is a pretty healthy breed. However, they can still have some plaque issue which is normally inherited by him Pomeranian parent. To keep your Pomsky healthy, you will want to make frequent trips to the veterinarian for annual check-ups at the very least. You will want to make sure you keep you Pomsky on a healthy diet.

Also, in order to keep your Pomsky happy and healthy, you will want to keep a good exercise regimen for your Pomsky. Pomskies are very active dogs with a lot of energy. In order to remain healthy, they need a lot of exercise. You can try to work on exercising your Pomsky by taking him on walks regularly. You may also consider running with your Pomsky, if you like to run yourself. A lot of play time is also a good way to exercise your Pomsky. Also, having a yard that your Pomsky is free to run around in will help to keep your Pomsky healthy.

Ultimately, Pomskies are a pretty healthy breed, as we currently know. The breed is still relatively new so its overall healthiness is not completely well known. But, in order to raise a happy and healthy Pomsky, you will need to stay up to date on vet visits, maintain a healthy diet, and keep your Pomsky well exercised.

# Common Diseases

Being such a new breed, Pomskies' health issues are not entirely known. However, it is understood that Pomskies have similar health issues as Pomeranians and Siberian Huskies, such as dental problems.

Siberian Huskies are generally healthy dogs, however, there are still some common ailments found in the breed. Before purchasing your Pomsky, you will want ot check with the breeder to be sure that the parents of the puppy you are planning on purchasing are clear of health issues.

Photo: Makala Braun

Siberian Huskies are known for suffering from hip dysplasia, elbow dysplasia, hypothyroidism, and von Willebrand's disease. Siberian Huskies are also known to suffer from cataracts, which are a film over the eye that makes it hard to see. They eyes will look cloudy. Cataracts usually occurs in old age and can be surgically removed. Cataracts can impair vision.

Siberian Huskies also suffer from Corneal Dystrophy which affects the cornea of the eye. It causes the lipids collecting in the cornea. It is normally noticeable in young adults and more common in females. There is no cure but it does not affect the dog's vision. Progressive Retinal Atrophy (PRA) is also found in Siberian Huskies. It is an eye disorder that can cause blindness. It is a loss of photoreceptors at the back of the eye. Dogs can do well if they are blinded by PRA but can use their other senses to compensate easily. It is detectable well before the dog can show any signs of blindness.

Pomeranians also are generally healthy dogs, but have a laundry list of possible common ailments. Pomeranians are known for their dental issues such as a buildup of plaque. Pomeranians can also suffer from teeth and gum issues as well as early tooth loss. Regular tooth exams are recommended.

Pomeranians can also suffer from a series of contact and food allergies. Noticeable signs to look for are licking of the paws or extensive rubbing of the face. When you notice these signs you should take your dog to the veterinarian. Pomeranians can also suffer from epilepsy. Eye problems such as cataracts, dry eye, and problems with their eye ducts are also common. This can cause blindness and you will want to seek help from your veterinarian.

Pomeranians can also suffer from hip dysplasia which is a genetic deformity of the hip joint. Also involving the hip joint is Legg-Perthes Disease, common in toy breeds like the Pomeranian.

Photo: Margaret Schmucker

Also common in Pomeranians is patellar luxation which is the dislocation of the knee cap. It can be crippling but not life threatening. A collapsed trachea is also dangerous for Pomeranians and possibly Pomskies as it blocks off easy air flow. Signs of a collapsed trachea are a dry cough sounding a lot like a goose honk. It is normally caused by pulling too hard on the collar. You may want to use a harness for your Pomeranian, or your Pomsky instead of the collar. Training your puppy to walk beside to you is also helpful. A collapse trachea can be treated.

Again, as there is not much yet known about Pomskies and their health histories, much of it has to be inferred by what the parent breeds commonly suffer from. When looking to purchase a Pomsky, you want to look into finding a Pomsky born from parents with healthy backgrounds. Reputable breeders should provide you with all of the proper paperwork for your Pomsky. This paperwork will include health records. This will help you to ensure that you will be raising a happy and healthy Pomsky.

# CHAPTER 14

# It All Comes Together

## Conclusion

The Pomsky is an adorable breed that many hopeful dog owners want to bring home as their own forever friend. Pomskies are a new designer breed of dog bred from a Siberian Husky mother and a Pomeranian father. This combination can create an adorably small Siberian Husky looking dog that has captured the hearts of many. There is not much known about these breeds right now. However, that does not keep many from wanting to learn more about this amazing new breed. These dogs can vary greatly in appearance, size, and temperament, most of which are inherited by the Pomsky parents.

They are very intelligent dogs that can learn quickly but can also be extremely stubborn in some cases, especially if they inherit the Pomeranian stubbornness. Although training your Pomsky puppy can be a challenge, if you are tenacious, patient, firm, and kindhearted to your adorable new friend, you can be successful in training your Pomsky. This training will help to forge an unbreakable bond between you and your Pomsky, so make it count and make it fun.

So, congratulations, dear reader. You are on your way to raising a loving and loyal companion. It is a lot of responsibility to care for and to train a young Pomsky, however the rewards will make it worth it in the end. Enjoy the time you spend with your new Pomsky puppy!

# GLOSSARY

**Alpha** - the individual that is in charge of the pack.

**American Kennel Club** - a registry of all purebred dog pedigrees for the United States, as they recognize them.

**Arachnids** - an animal class, includes spiders and scorpioins

**Canine Hepatitis** - viral infection that causes an inflammation of the liver.

**Canine Parvovirus** - a class of small viruses that affects animals and causes contagious diseases, especially in dogs.

**Chukchi** - an ancient Siberian hunting people

**Designer Dog Breed** - a cross between two purebred dogs

**Distemper** - viral disease, common in dogs that causes fever, coughing, and catarrh

**Double-Layered Coat (Double Coat)** - a coat on a dog made up of a top coat and under coat

**Microchipping** - implanting a microchip under the skin of the dog in order to be able to identify your puppy.

**Outer Layer** - also referred to as a top coat, it is the fur on the outermost layer of the dog's double coat

**Parasites** - an organism that lives in or on another organism and feeds off of the host.

**Parent Club** - a club specified for a specific breed, normally accepted by the AKC

**Piloerection** - involuntary reaction in which the hair stands on end, triggered by cold, shock, or fright.

**Pomsky Club of America** - a club that is looking to get the Pomsky accepted by the AKC as a registered purebred dog breed.

**Rabies** - contagious and fatal viral disease that causes madness and convulsions, transmitted by saliva, can be transmitted to humans.

**Small Dog Syndrome** - a set of unwanted behaviors that are normally displayed by smaller dogs when they want to demonstrate who is the boss.

**Undercoat** - also referred to as an inner coat, the coat that is under the longer hair (top coat), soft and dense

# References

"All About the Pomsky." Pet360. Pet360 Inc, 2015. Web. 14
    Oct. 2015. <http://www.pet360.com/dog/breeds/
    all-about-the-pomsky/nhUHXQq3qk2slwBgJO0Jiw>.

Alling, Meredith. "Your Puppy's First Vet Visit." PetCareRx. PetPlus,
    2 Mar. 2014. Web. 31 Oct. 2015. <http://www.petcar-
    erx.com/article/your-puppys-first-vet-visit/1694>.

"Approved PCA Breeders." Pomsky Club of America. Pomsky Club
    of America, 2014. Web. 25 Oct. 2015. <http://www.pomsky-
    clubofamerica.org/#!approved-breeders/ca4p>.

Benal, Jolanta, CPDT-KA, CBCC-KA. "How to Socialize Your Puppy."
    Quick and Dirty Tips. Macmillan Holdings, LLC, 29 July 2014.
    Web. 02 Nov. 2015. <http://www.quickanddirtytips.com/
    pets/dog-behavior/how-to-socialize-your-puppy>.

Benal, Jolanta, CPDT-KA, CBCC-KA. "Teach Your Dog to Give or Drop
    an Item." Quick and Dirty Tips. Macmillan Holdings, LLC, 13 Jan.
    2015. Web. 2 Nov. 2015. <http://www.quickanddirtytips.com/pets/
    dog-behavior/teach-your-dog-to-give-or-drop-an-item>.

Brecher, Stacey. "How to Set Boundaries With Your Dog." The Dog Daily. Studio
    One, 2015. Web. 31 Oct. 2015. <http://www.thedogdaily.com/ca/hap-
    py/play/set_boundaries_for_your_dog/index.html#.Vja-mLerTIU>.

"Bringing a New Puppy Home." RaisingSpot.com: Your Insider's Guide to
    Four-Legged Friends. RaisingSpot.com, 2015. Web. 23 Oct. 2015.
    <http://www.raisingspot.com/intro-bringing-puppy-home>.

"Bringing Your New Puppy Home." Dog House Chatter. Nylabone,
    20 May 2011. Web. 16 Oct. 2015. <http://www.nylabone.com/
    dog-house-chatter/2011/05/20/bringing-your-new-puppy-home/>.

"Dog Bite Prevention." RaisingSpot.com: Your Insider's Guide to Four-
    Legged Friends. RaisingSpot.com, 2015. Web. 31 Oct. 2015. <http://
    www.raisingspot.com/adopting/dog-bite-prevention>.

Dolce, Jessica. "Peace in the Yard: 7 Ways To Dog Proof Your Fence." Notes from
    a Dog Walker: Stories from the Sidewalk. N.p., 08 Aug. 2013. Web. 30 Oct.
    2015. <http://notesfromadogwalker.com/2013/08/08/dog-fence-fixes/>.

Dunbar, Dr. Ian. *"What Makes a Good Puppy Class?"* Dog Star Daily. Jeneration Web Development, 5 Jan. 2009. Web. 27 Oct. 2015. <http://www.dog-stardaily.com/training/what-makes-good-puppy-class-dr-ian-dunbar>.

Eapen, Deepak. *"5 Useful Positive Reinforcement House and Potty Training Tips for Your Dog."* Eapen's Blog on Pets and Animals. N.p., 15 July 2011. Web. 02 Nov. 2015. <http://raisingpetsandanimals.blogspot.com/2011/07/5-useful-positive-reinforcement-house.html>.

Gabriel, Madeline. *"How Can I Socialize My Puppy With Kids?"* Dogs and Babies RSS. N.p., 3 Aug. 2012. Web. 02 Nov. 2015. <http://www.dogsandbabieslearning.com/2012/08/03/how-can-i-socialize-my-puppy-with-kids/>.

Gest, Jason. *"List of Pomsky Breeders Worldwide | Cute Pomsky."* Cute Pomsky. Cute Pomsky, 2015. Web. 25 Oct. 2015. <http://po-meranian-husky.com/list-of-pomsky-breeders/>.

Gest, Jason. *"Pomeranian Husky FAQS | Cute Pomsky."* Cute Pomsky. Cute Pomsky, 1 Sept. 2015. Web. 22 Oct. 2015. <http://pomeranian-husky.com/pomsky-faq/>.

Gest, Jason. *"4 Questions to Ask Before Purchasing a Pomsky | Cute Pomsky."* Cute Pomsky. Cute Pomsky, 7 June. 2014. Web. 22 Oct. 2015. <http://pomeranian-husky.com/4-questions-to-ask-before-purchasing-a-pomsky/>.

Gest, Jason. *"5 Essential Pet Supplies To Have When Bringing Your New Pomsky Puppies Home | Cute Pomsky."* Cute Pomsky. Cute Pomsky, 9 Jan. 2015. Web. 22 Oct. 2015. <http://pomeranian-husky.com/5-essential-pet-sup-plies-to-have-when-bringing-your-new-pomsky-puppies-home/>.

Griffiths, Stephanie. *"Grooming Your Pomsky."* Moonlit Pomskys - A UK Pomsky Breeder. Moonlit Pomskys, 8 Oct. 2014. Web. 03 Nov. 2015. <http://www.moonlitpomskys.com/#!Grooming-your-Pomsky/cyh4/9F8F1479-DAAA-4B5C-B5B0-E39B0C7D3A56>.

Hillestad, Katharine, DVM. *"Puppy Proofing Your Home and Providing a Safe Environment."* Puppy Proofing Your Home and Providing a Safe Environment. Drs. Foster & Smith Veterinary Services Department, n.d. Web. 26 Oct. 2015. <http://www.peted-ucation.com/article.cfm?c=2%2B2106&aid=3283>.

*"History."* My Husky. N.p., 28 Aug. 2010. Web. 19 Oct. 2015. <http://www.myhusky.com.au/history/>.

*"History of the Pomsky Breed, Caring for Pomsky Pups."* Perfect
Pomskies. Marketing-crew.com, 2015. Web. 22 Oct. 2015.
<http://www.perfectpomskies.com/about/>.

*"How to Teach Your Dog Basic Commands."* The Humane Society
of the United States. The Humane Society, 29 Aug. 2014.
Web. 2 Nov. 2015. <http://www.humanesociety.org/ani-
mals/dogs/tips/teaching_basic_commands.html>.

*How to Train a Dog to "Heel"* (K9-1.com). YouTube. YouTube, 23 Dec. 2013. Web.
03 Nov. 2015. <https://www.youtube.com/watch?v=u9cpD6VFhTU>.

Martin, Debbie. *"Where's the Potty? How to House Train Your Puppy."*
Karen Pryor. Clicker Training, 04 Jan. 2013. Web. 02 Nov.
2015. <http://www.clickertraining.com/node/3892>.

Millan, Cesar. *"Teaching the 'sit' Command." Cesar's Way.* Cesar's Way
Inc., 17 June 2015. Web. 02 Nov. 2015. <https://www.cesar-
sway.com/dog-training/obedience/the-sit-command>.

Paxton Ladd, Lorna. *"The Importance of Setting Boundaries with Your New
Puppy."* Ruff Ideas. Word Press and Stargazer, 14 Feb. 2014. Web.
15 Oct. 2015. <http://www.happytailsspa-blog.com/2014/02/14/
the-importance-of-setting-boundaries-with-your-new-puppy/>.

*"Pomeranian."* Dogtime. TotallyHer Medica, LLC, an Evolve Media, LLC Company,
2015. Web. 19 Oct. 2015. <http://dogtime.com/dog-breeds/pomeranian>.

*"Pomsky."* Dog Breed Plus. N.p., 2015. Web. 22 Oct. 2015. <http://
www.dogbreedplus.com/dog_breeds/pomsky.php>.

*"Pomsky."* PetGuide.com. Vertical Scope Inc., 2013. Web. 15 Oct.
2015. <http://www.petguide.com/breeds/dog/pomsky/>.

*"Pomsky Headquarters - Your Source for Pomsky Information."*
Pomsky Headquarters. N.p., 19 Mar. 2013. Web.
18 Oct. 2015. <http://pomskyhq.com/>.

*"Pomsky Puppy Training."* Pomsky Pals. Wish SEO, 19 Mar. 2015. Web. 22 Oct.
2015. <http://pomskypals.com/pomsky/pomsky-puppy-training/>.

*"Pomsky 101 Archives."* The Pomeranian Husky. Up, 2015. Web. 28 Oct. 2015.
<http://www.thepomeranianhusky.com/category/pomsky-101/>.

*"Q and A."* Pomsky Club of America. Pomsky Club of America, 2014. Web. 25
Oct. 2015. <http://www.pomskyclubofamerica.org/#!qanda/c20r9>.

*"Setting Rules for Dogs and Kids."* RaisingSpot.com: Your Insider's Guide to Four-Legged Friends. RaisingSpot.com, 2015. Web. 31 Oct. 2015. <http://www.raisingspot.com/adopting/buy-puppy-for-a-child>.

*"Siberian Husky."* Dogtime. TotallyHer Medica, LLC, an Evolve Media, LLC Company, 2015. Web. 21 Oct. 2015. <http://dogtime.com/dog-breeds/siberian-husky>.

*"Siberian Husky Dog Breed Information."* - American Kennel Club. AKC Global Services, 2015. Web. 19 Oct. 2015. <http://www.akc.org/dog-breeds/siberian-husky/>.

*"Socializing Your Puppy."* ASPCA. The American Society for the Prevention of Cruelty to Animals, n.d. Web. 01 Nov. 2015. <https://www.aspca.org/pet-care/virtual-pet-behaviorist/dog-behavior/socializing-your-puppy>.

*"Socializing with Other Dogs."* Pet Care Article. PetCo, n.d. Web. 02 Nov. 2015. <http://www.petco.com/Content/ArticleList/Article/30/1/290/Socializing-with-Other-Dogs.aspx>.

*"Teaching Dogs the "Come" Command."* RSS. The Humane Society, 30 Jan. 2015. Web. 02 Nov. 2015. <http://www.humanesociety.org/animals/dogs/tips/teaching_come_command.html?referrer=https%3A%2F%2Fwww.google.com%2F>.

*"Teaching Your Dog Not to Pull on a Leash."* ASPCA. The American Society for the Prevention of Cruelty to Animals, n.d. Web. 3 Nov. 2015. <https://www.aspca.org/pet-care/virtual-pet-behaviorist/dog-behavior/teaching-your-dog-not-pull-leash>.

*"Teaching Your Dog to "Leave It""* ASPCA. The American Society for the Prevention of Cruelty to Animals, n.d. Web. 03 Nov. 2015. <https://www.aspca.org/pet-care/virtual-pet-behaviorist/dog-behavior/teaching-your-dog-leave-it>.

*"Teaching Your Dog to Lie Down."* ASPCA. The American Society for the Prevention of Cruelty to Animals, n.d. Web. 02 Nov. 2015. <https://www.aspca.org/pet-care/virtual-pet-behaviorist/dog-behavior/teaching-your-dog-lie-down>.

*"Teaching Your Dog to Sit."* ASPCA. The American Society for the Prevention of Cruelty to Animals, n.d. Web. 02 Nov. 2015. <https://www.aspca.org/pet-care/virtual-pet-behaviorist/dog-behavior/teaching-your-dog-sit>.

*"Teaching Your Dog to Stay."* ASPCA. The American Society for the Prevention of Cruelty to Animals, n.d. Web. 02 Nov. 2015. <https://www.aspca.org/pet-care/virtual-pet-behaviorist/dog-behavior/teaching-your-dog-stay>.

*"The Differences Between Fleas and Ticks."* Cesar's Way. Cesar's Way Inc., 17 June 2015. Web. 03 Nov. 2015. <https://www.cesarsway.com/dog-care/flea-and-tick/the-differences-between-fleas-and-ticks>.

*"The Pomeranian Husky."* The Pomeranian Husky. Up, 2015. Web. 28 Oct. 2015. <http://www.thepomeranianhusky.com/>.

*"Top 10 Qualities of a Great Veterinarian."* Veterinary Schools. Education. org, n.d. Web. 03 Nov. 2015. <http://veterinaryschools.com/resources/top-10-qualities-of-a-great-veterinarian>.

*"Vaccinations."* ASPCA. The American Society for the Prevention of Cruelty to Animals, n.d. Web. 03 Nov. 2015. <https://www.aspca.org/pet-care/dog-care/vaccinations>.

Wall, Janet, and Rick Wall. *"Teaching "Off!""* Love Your Dog. N.p., n.d. Web. 03 Nov. 2015. <http://www.loveyourdog.com/off.html>.

Welton, Roger, Dr. *"10 Household Items That Must Be Kept Out of Reach of Dogs."* Web DVM. Web-DVM. net, 2015. Web. 26 Oct. 2015. <http://web-dvm.net/10-household-items-that-must-be-kept-out-of-reach-of-dogs/>.

Wilson, Sara Logan. *"What Foods Are Toxic for Dogs."* CanineJournal. com. Cover Story Media, Inc., 20 Dec. 2008. Web. 28 Oct. 2015. <http://www.caninejournal.com/foods-not-to-feed-dog/>.

Wilson, Sarah. *"The 4 Most Important Pet Dog Qualities."* Sarah Wilson: Dog Expert. Win Win Media LLC., 21 July 2013. Web. 25 Oct. 2015. <https://sarahwilsondogexpert.com/the-4-most-important-pet-dog-qualities/>.

Woolf, Norma Bennett. *"Hidden Fences."* Dog Owner's Guide. Canis Major Publications, 2014. Web. 27 Oct. 2015. <http://www.canismajor.com/dog/fences1.html>.

Yin, Sophia, DVM. *"Dog Training: Operant Conditioning."* The Bark. The Bark, Inc., n.d. Web. 02 Nov. 2015. <http://the-bark.com/content/dog-training-operant-conditioning>.

Made in the USA
Middletown, DE
28 October 2018